Homo sapiens A Liberal's Perspective

Ron Newby

ISBN: 0615970095
ISBN 13: 9780615970097
Library of Congress Control Number: 2014903417
Ron Newby, Del Mar, CA

Acknowledgments

THERE ARE MANY people who have added to my understanding and appreciation for science and the humanities, individuals that have instilled the skill of rational thought, who have lead me to do deep thinking. I am very appreciative that the following have been part of my education: my Pasadena High School Botany teacher, Mr. Ball, many Professors at the University of California, Santa Barbara, including Dr. Garret Hardin for his understanding of man's place in the universe, Drs. Bob Haller and Wally Muller my Botany professors and my thesis advisor, Dr. Eduardo Orias. Professors at The Salk Institute who have inspired me have been Dr. Jacob Bronowski, a polymath, the humanist Dr. Jonas Salk, Dr. Francis Crick, Nobel Laureate, a brilliant critical thinker and Dr. Roger Guillemin, Nobel Laureate and artist. Conversations with friends have helped in formulating ideas: Robert Poe, Dolores Welty and Murray Powers.

I would like to acknowledge and thank the individuals who have read and made helpful suggestions for this manuscript: Dr. David Schubert, Jeanne Cretois-Burk, Michael Parr, Mark Stabb and especially Beverly Boggs, my partner whose encouragement has sustained me.

Quotation are from a variety of sources, including author's words as published, and

www.brainyquote.com
www.goodreads.com/quotes
http://www.searchquotes.com

Contents

1

The Beginning

IT STARTED WITH a bang, a really big bang. And then, 13.8 billion years later, here we are. Human's long journey took us out of Africa, to caves and onto the Fertile Crescent of Mesopotamia between the Tigris and Euphrates rivers, the cradle of civilization. The Greeks, the Romans, the Age of Enlightenment, the Industrial Revolution, the American Revolution, the French Revolution, George Washington, Abraham Lincoln and Barack Obama. There, you have it; the history of man. Human history, excessively oversimplified. We humans did it all and we did it because we are the masters of our universe. Humans are special, we are unique, and not at all like the other animals that roam the earth. We added an 'e' to indicate our uniqueness; we are humane.

Needless to say, this accounting of humans is whimsical. There have been over a dozen other species of the genus *Homo* that didn't make it to the 21st century. How did it happen that we, *Homo sapiens*, are the last *Hominin* species remaining.

Hominin is a primate of a family *Hominidae* that includes humans and their fossil ancestors. *Homo* is our genus and includes other members of the human clade after the split from the tribe *Panini* (chimpanzees). Our scientific name is *Homo sapiens*. We have evolved from ancient *hominins*, and our behaviors are similar to behaviors of our ancient ancestors. We are primates with an intellect.

Our behaviors have evolved from the brain of our *hominin* ancestors; the brain they developed and forwarded on to us. The condensed version: We are tribal animals. We are *Homo sapiens*. Early man roamed a pristine planet. We now find ourselves on a planet that is less than pristine, suffering from overpopulation and a worsening climate. The rich are getting richer and the poor are growing in numbers. Humans are certainly marvelous, but our politics, religion and a few of our atrocious behaviors are contributing to the possibility of our downfall. Humans have enslaved, tortured, waged war and polluted the earth. The earth is warming. Alarming is the lack of concern and understanding among most individuals to our worsening environment. Is our destructive nature cause for concern? Do we truly have Free Will? Should we now be more concerned with our legacy or with our obituary? What can be done, if anything? Are there feasible alternatives? This will be a critique of humans, their history, their trait and behaviors, their constructs, politics and religions. There will always be a bias to any evaluation or critique and this will declaratively be from a liberal's perspective.

There are prevalent assumptions that man can solve any problem. Often heard is that *we* are human. No problem is beyond solution or *they* will find the answer and fix the problem. What I heard 50 years ago concerning Over Population - *"we'll just head off into space and find another planet."* Now that we have a climate crisis, the often heard response now seems to be: *"no problem at all, warm weather will be a welcome change from those awful winters."* Well, people, those answers are not realistic. How did we get in this mess and what can we do about it?

I will attempt to make the argument that we are animals and thus are similar in many ways to all the other animals. However, unlike all the other animals, we have the ability to destroy our environment and humans as well. Humans have at times been inhumane. Our political system may be the cause to many problems. We have the instincts that we receive from our ancestors. Our brain is the decider of our behavior and that our artificial institutions are partly to blame. Humans are unique in that we are creative and have the intellect to understand future problems and to possibly change our behaviors. We can become a more nobel species.

"Why can't we all get along?", was spoken by Rodney King, after being brutalized by the police. Why do some of us behave badly while others are "saints"? Can *Homo sapiens* behave smartly? We're here in the 21st century with a bright future. Is the future that bright?

First, *Full Disclosure.* I have had a liberal education, I tend to read nonfiction, I am a biologist, an artist, a liberal and an atheist; a nonconformist, maybe an outsider.

I was born in 1938 and I have had a marvelous and extremely interesting life. I grew up in Pasadena and Monterey, California. When I was 10 years old my father passed and subsequently, my youth revolved around my participation in the Boy Scouts. I was exposed to the outdoors; camping, hiking, campfires and the opportunity to rely on outdoor skills to have a great time. I always had great admiration of the natural world. Memorable was my high school Botany class and my teacher, Mr. Ball. He inspired his students to wonder, ask questions and find answers to what life was. Life in the biological sense; how did plant grow and reproduce and what cellular structures and mechanism were responsible for growth? I was not indoctrinated with religious beliefs; that I believe was good fortune. I attended The University of California, Santa Barbara where I received a liberal education. I received a Bachelor of Arts degree in Botany and a Master of Arts degree in Analytical Biology. Following, I spent 27 years as a researcher at The Salk Institute in La Jolla, CA., studying gene regulation; how genes, at the molecular level, are turned on and off in response to environmental factors.

While at The Salk Institute, I had numerous conversations with some great thinkers including Jonas Salk, Jacob Bronowski and Francis Crick, all three greatly influenced my life and were influential towards my writing this essay.

Jonas Salk, (1914 - 1995) was the discoverer of the "Salk Polio Vaccine" as well as founder of the world famous The Salk Institute for Biological Studies. Dr. Salk described The Institute as *"a crucible for creativity."*

Jacob Bronowski (1908 - 1974) was a British mathematician, biologist, humanist and an associate director of the Salk Institute for Biological Studies from 1964. He is the author of the book The Ascent of Man as well as the BBC and PBS television series of the same name.

Francis Crick (1916 - 2004), Nobel Laureate. He was a biophysicist, a neuroscientist and contributed to our understanding of human consciousness. Crick together with James Watson co-discovered the structure of DNA in 1953. He was a Distinguished Professor at The Salk Institute.

I am the founder and director of *The Bronowski Art&Science Forum.* Art and science are both creative expressions of human imagination. The Forum has been a crucible for conversations between individuals from disparate disciplines: artists and scientists. The Forum attempts in a modest way to maintain the sensibility of Jacob Bronowski's and Jonas Salk's original idea of the shared commonalities of art and of science. Since 1999, there has been 121 Forums. The format of The Forum is to host a single topic conversation between an artist and a scientist; each offering their perspective.

The titles of several previous Forums have been: *"Aesthetic, Experience, and Inquiry"* with artist Jennifer Steinkamp and Psychologist Piotr Winkielman.

"Making Sense of Space: Sculpture, Mind and Human Imagination" with cognitive scientist Rafael Nunez, and artist Jennifer Pastor. *"Blurred Lines: Art, Architecture and the Cognitive Sciences"* with cognitive scientist David Kirsh and architect Jennifer Luce.

"The Mind's Eye: Perspectives from Art History and Visual Neuroscience" with Neuroscientist Richard Krauzlis and art historian Jack Greenstein. Complete programming may be found at the website: www.BronowskiForum.org.

The conversations of the over 100 outstanding artists and scientists that have made presentations at The Forum, has been the inspiration for this book.

Curiosity seems to be my nature. I ask questions, often where no answer is yet available. With all these years spent studying, with wonder and awe of the earth and all the life forms, I ponder the state of man and his affairs. I now find myself here and now writing down my observations, conjectures, thoughts and ideas; not theories. I do have great concern that we may not be able to stave off our possible demise. I am not a specialist, not an expert in the topics that I present. I'm a generalist and I think this allows me to have a rather broad and unique perspective as to the nature of *Homo sapiens.*

I am a practicing artist and have studied art history most of my life. Both activities have brought to me great satisfaction. I often visit art museums and look carefully at selected artworks. One of my most admired artists is Pablo Picasso, not because his paintings fetch huge sums of money but because he saw reality in a much different manner. He explored the world with an artist's eye. He painted the human subject, usually women, from several perspectives simultaneously, whereas his predecessors had not. Picasso realized that one could depict these women from a side and frontal perspective in one composition. Information that is greater than a depiction of just one side. His paintings, some of which were done in a hurried "frenzy", so to speak, were worked over several times. One can notice that one color was laid down; he must have stepped back to examine what he had done, and not satisfied, added another color on top of the previous color. He didn't bother to completely mask the first paint marks applied, but hurrying on to the next paint stroke. He worked rapidly, as rapidly as his mind would allow. If one inspects his linear sketches, one realizes that a simple flowing gestural line conveys the essence; our brain fill in the detail, easily. I marvel at the plasticity of his mind. Picasso observed and expressed the world quite a bit differently than most others.

That which is most exasperating to me are phrases dealing with man's invulnerability. "*Man is special, we aren't animals. We can do anything if we set our minds to it. It's all a part of God's plan. Don't worry.*" In one sense we are special, not at all like animals. In another sense we are not all that special; we're just like the other animals. We are one species; one of over sixteen million other species of plants and animals living on earth. We have traits that have their origins far back in our evolutionary history and we have traits that are uniquely human. We have been honed by tens of thousands of years of selection for traits that were of survival value. Some of our behaviors may be beneficial for our survival; others neutral and a few of our behaviors may contribute to our demise. What we believe and how we act are functions of our history, our brain and our behavior; a consequence of our being *Homo sapiens.* All human behaviors originate in our brains. Our brain is the source, the decider for the path we take.

The word "Human" can be emotionally charged. It is fraught with context and inferences, and as such, I wish to avoid this word to some extent. The term *Homo sapiens* is neutral and free of emotional content. It is the scientific name that has been assigned to us.

2

We Evolved

The Theory of Evolution

"One of the most frightening things in the Western world, and in this country in particular, is the number of people who believe in things that are scientifically false. If someone tells me that the earth is less than 10,000 years old, in my opinion he should see a psychiatrist."
FRANCIS CRICK

1925 WAS THE year of a famous American legal case referred to as *"The Scopes Monkey Trial."* John Scopes, a Tennessee high school teacher was accused of teaching evolution in violation of the Butler Act, a Tennessee law prohibiting public school teachers from denying the Biblical account of man's origin. Arguing for the prosecution was William Jennings Bryan, a devout Christian and a leading American politician. Clarence Darrow, a leading member of the American Civil Liberties Union argued for the defense. Scopes was found guilty and fined $100, but the verdict was overturned on a technicality.

Today, nearly 90 years post this trial, many US states are still contentiously debating whether Evolution or Creationism and Intelligent Design should be taught in public schools. The public seems divided. There are several recent polls asking Americans their beliefs on evolution, with quite similar results. A Gallup poll found that 46% believe God created humankind in a single day about 10,000 years ago, a literal interpretation of the Bible. Just 15 percent say humans evolved without the assistance of God. The poll was conducted by interviewing a random sample of 1,012 adults, aged 18 and older, living in all 50 U.S. states and the District of Columbia. Another poll by YouGov, a nonpartisan organization, found that 40% favor teaching creationism and intelligent design in schools. 21% say humans evolved without the involvement of God.

We think of ourselves as rational intelligent beings. From my perspective, this is alarming. It speaks to the inadequacies of our educational system and to the influence of religion in public policy. I'm astounded that a huge percentage of the population does not believe in evolution. These Bible-believers seem to either lack adequate education or they have been seduced (I think this word is appropriate) by the influence of religion.

While school boards and religious groups grabble with issues of what sort of science, fiction or nonfiction, should be taught, I would like to refresh my readers on Evolution Theory including the evolutionary history of *Homo sapiens*. I have always believed in evolution. Considering the complexity and the similarities that animals and plants share, it just makes sense.

We are just one of millions of species on earth and the *Theory of Evolution* is a rational method to explain the great variety of species that have inhabited earth. The theory offers explanations to how life forms arose, the lineages and the mechanisms that produce such diversity. The theory of evolution is the history of man and all organisms, past and present. The theory relies only upon evidence. It is devoid of moral or ethical principles. It does not offer direction nor a purpose of life. Religion is one, but not the only, source for moral and ethical guidance.

Charles Darwin in his 1859 book, On the Origin of Species outlined the theory of evolution, a scientific theory that explains the diversity of life forms and the mechanism that created this diversity, *Natural Selection*.

In his travels and his study of nature he observed that species produced offspring in numbers greater than just simple replacement; that of all the offspring each pair produced, only two on average survived. He also noticed that there was variation among the progeny, not all were absolutely identical. He was very familiar with the popular activity of plant and animal breeding, where enthusiasts would select for breeding a specimen with favored traits. He did not know about DNA, but he did understand that traits were inherited and that if an individual was born with a trait that offered a survival or reproductive advantage, even a very slight advantage, the statistical odds were that this trait would be passed on down through generations. He also observed that these modified traits appeared randomly and that most changes were deleterious, that runts may appear in a litter. On occasion, a trait would arise that offered a slight biological advantage to that organism. From his geology knowledge, he knew that the environment is not static, that the earth's topography and climates were diverse and that both changed over time.

With this broad knowledge, he postulated the encompassing theory of evolution and natural selection; nature's way of selecting the more fit individuals; *survival of the fittest.*

Darwin provided very strong evidence for man's common ancestry with the living apes, and that all human populations were more closely related to each other than to any living primate; they were the same species. Concerning humans, Darwin drew evidence for our having evolved from three main categories; similarities between humans and other primates, similarities in embryological development, and vestigial organs referencing the Emu, a flightless bird with wings that seemed not fit for flight.

As an example of evolution; if among a brood of chicks, one individual was hatched having a slightly longer beak, or perhaps a stronger beak, that individual may have the ability to reach further down into a flower to extract just a bit more nectar, or if a stronger beak, to crack open more seeds, or crack them open more quickly, and thus get more food per day. A bit of advantage that could assist that individual to survive and hence reproduce.

When I see all the vibrant colors of flowers in my garden, I am in awe. There are flowers displaying characteristics that attract the pollinators, bees, insects and birds which have the visual acuity to detect the flowers. What a marvelous example of both evolution and of symbiosis.

Considering the overwhelming scientific evidence that has been published in peer reviewed journals, *Homo sapiens* did evolve from more primitive life forms and these more primitive forms themselves evolved from a primordial cocktail, the results of which were natural chemical reactions. The most learned scholars accept that we are the product of evolutionary processes and that we have retained some, maybe even a great abundance of those traits that developed in earlier primates. If you honestly believe that The Theory of Evolution is *just* a *theory*, then hold out at arm's length, an egg, palm side down. Open your hand; then tell me that Sir Isaac Newton's *Theory of Gravity* is *just* a *theory*.

"The Universe seems neither benign nor hostile, merely indifferent."
CARL SAGAN

Present day *Homo sapiens* have the advantage, thanks to the scholars and scientists that preceded us, to find answers to questions, free from mystical folklore and religious explanations. We are free to be rational rather than accept answers that come from ancient writings, written when man was pre-enlightened, before the age of scientific scholarship. It may be arduous to read sections of this book, but I think it is necessary to appreciate our present condition. We can make judgements based on rational thought given we have the appropriate information.

Our Evolutionary path

If you do not have a background in paleoanthropology, you may find the following helpful. However, if you are a paleoanthropologist, you may find the following simplistic and missing a great amount of rather significant detail. For ease of reading, I will follow a simpler path. The point here is that humans have a long and continuous history; there is no "Missing Link."

My focus will be on the Animal Kingdom, excluding the Plant Kingdom as its relevance is less important for my personal view. I do acknowledge that plants have played a very significant role in human evolution and their evolution is quite similar in principle. The Plant Kingdom has followed a very complex evolutionary path, which led to this diverse world of plants. I don't expect you to memorize this material, nor will there be a quiz following. I will just provide a survey to refresh for you our evolutionary history.

I want to point out that references may be fewer in this section than one would expect in scientific peer reviewed papers. For additional material, I suggest that *Wikipedia* is an excellent first step. The articles contained therein are well referenced and often contain photos of reconstructed early man. Other website references I would suggest are: evolutionpages.com, humanorigins, si.edu, talkorigins.org and australianmuseum.net.au.

We humans are at the end of one twig on the Tree of Life, a tree which has millions of branches and twigs. The origins of life go well beyond the Tree of Life to the origin of the universe. The universe is estimated to be about 13.8 billion years old, whereas the earth was formed about 4.54 billion years ago. A considerable period of time. To assist in comprehending these enormous lengths of time, consider that one billion years is 1,000 million years.

The first billion years of earth's existence, the planet was lifeless. The earliest life on earth existed at least 3.5 billions years ago. At that time, the earth's atmosphere was composed primarily of methane, ammonia, water, hydrogen sulfide, carbon monoxide, carbon dioxide and phosphate. Oxygen was either rare or absent. It has been demonstrated in the laboratory that an electrical discharge, lightening, into a chamber containing these early earth molecules can catalyze the synthesis of basic bio-molecules such as amino acids, which are the building blocks of proteins and phospholipids which are the component of cell membranes and nucleotides which could form more complex ribonucleic acid molecules. No one to date has yet synthesized a "protocell" using these basic components, however there is current research. I would predict success within a few years. The creation of a new life form in the laboratory may prove to have serious ethical questions.

There is another very interesting alternative hypothesis, yet unproven, that suggests that Mars is the site of the origin of life, specifically ribonucleic acid (RNA). There were conditions and inorganic chemicals on that planet conducive to the synthesis of RNA; borate and molybdate that could acted as a catalysis, binding the precursors of RNA thus aiding the assembly and formation of more complex RNA molecules which could proceed on to form DNA molecules. A giant meteor impacting Mars could have kicked up debris containing these precursors which, by gradational forces landed upon earth.

Regardless of the actual origin of life here on earth, Eukaryotes, cells with nuclei, first appeared about 2.1 billion years ago. During the past billion years, the earth has gone through numerous thermal changes, extended periods of cold climate followed by warmer interglacial periods. Even the global location of the continents has drastically changed positions. One billion years ago and again 600 million years ago and the latest, 240 millions years ago the continents were not separated as they are today. At each of these periods there was but one supercontinent, followed by continental drift and separation into 'sub continents'. The latest continental shift commenced about 200 million years ago as the supercontinent, named Pangaea, split apart into various land masses and drifted at very slow rates to what we now recognize as the present positions of the seven continents.

The present rate of our tectonic drift is slow, very slow. Europe is drifting away from North America on tectonic plates at a rate of one inch per year. Ever since the Precambrian (600 million years ago), ice ages or glacial ages have occurred at widely spaced intervals of geologic time—approximately 200 million years—lasting for millions, or even tens of millions of years.

From the first occurrence of early eukaryote life forms, another 1.6 billion years (505 million years BP) were required for the first vertebrates to appear. (BP = Before Present) Mammals made their appearance 220 million years BP. Primates evolved about 75 - 85 million years BP. As you may recall, the age of dinosaurs was between 195 million years BP until the great extinction that occurred about 66 million years BP when a great asteroid crashed in the gulf of Mexico resulting in the demise of three-quarters of plant and animal species on Earth, including all non-avian dinosaurs. Some very small shrew-like primates species that dwelled subterraneanly survived feeding off the remains of decimated organisms. The small surviving very early primates went on to evolve into our branch of the tree of life. The following 50 million years after the asteroid incident, primates diversified into such groups as lemur, tarsiers, monkeys and apes.

During all periods of the earth's geological history, climate and the topography has been under constant change, some exceedingly slow, some events occurred more rapidly. During these periods of climatic change, life forms either adapted to the changes, migrated to areas not affected or perished.

The most recent ice age, more precisely Glacial Age, began 2.6 million years ago. Glacial ages are dynamic periods with glacial periods alternating with warm periods, called interglacial periods. These cycles occur on a time scale of 40,000 to 100,000 years. The earth is presently in an interglacial period which started about 10-13 thousand years ago. When the earth enters a glacial phase, polar ice accumulates and atmospheric water condenses to form snow and ice at the polar regions of earth and then subsequently the ice spreads out from the poles. Glaciation results in drier climate, tropical forests retreat being replaced by grasslands and eventually by desertification.

Factors which may contribute to these climatic changes include a complicated dynamic interaction between such events as solar intensity, tilting of the earth's axis, eccentricity of the earth's orbit, the distance of the earth from the sun, position and height of the continents, ocean circulation, and the composition of the atmosphere as well as catastrophic events such as asteroid impacts and volcanic activity. *Hominin's* evolution took place within a changing and challenging geological and climatic environment.

Presently there are about 18 known and described members from the tribe *Hominins*, the subfamily classification for members of the branch of primates after the split from the tribe Panini (chimpanzees). These known ancestors most likely do not include the total of other *hominin* species that participated in the history of human origins. While the record is incomplete, research is ongoing. Paleoanthropologists study early human fossil teeth and skeletal remains as well as found tools and evidence of tool making, fossilized footprints, traces of campfires, bones of animals digested and other food detritus. DNA evidence, computers and sophisticated mathematical models are used for tracking variables such as skull size or pelvic variations over time. Evolutionists estimate that humans separated from chimpanzees about 6 million years ago.

Chimpanzees, *Pan troglodytes* and Bonobos, *Pan paniscus, are* the closest living relatives to humans. A separate twig leads towards humans, *Homo sapiens.*

Near this split of *Pan* from *Homo* is the genus ***Ardipithecus***, with two known species representatives. There is however, ongoing scientific discussion whether *Ardititheus* was in the direct *Hominins* lineage as their physical appearance, as rendered by an artist, seem to have physical characteristics of both ape and early man; perhaps something in between, perhaps the "Missing Link" that deniers often mention.

Ardipithecus kadabba lived about 5.6 million years ago in Eastern Africa and had a brain size of 300 and 350 cubic centimeters (cm3). This species is known only from teeth, their wear pattern and smaller pieces of skeletal bones.

Ardipithecus ramidus roamed Africa about 4.4 million years ago. Compared to Chimpanzees whose feet are specialized for climbing, *A. ramidus'* feet were better suited for walking. The canine teeth of *A. ramidus* are smaller, and equal in size between males and females as compared with Apes. From this, researchers infer certain aspects of the social behavior of this species: reduced male-to-male conflict, increased pair-bonding, and increased parental investment; social behavior that arose before enlarged brains and stone tool usage. In 1994, paleontologists unearthed in Ethiopia, a relatively complete *A. ramidus* fossil skeleton of a female, nicknamed *"Ardi"*. She was estimated to have weighed 110 lbs. and stood 4 feet tall. Her brain size was about 325 cm3, similar to that of chimps.

A species of hominin, ***Kenyanthropus playtos,*** known from a fossilized specimen, roamed Kenya between 3.5 - 3.2 million years ago. Some scientists suggest that this species may be an ancestor to the genus *Homo.* This species was geographically and temporally similar to another species, *Australopithecus afarensis,* but is physically distinctive. It is believed both occupied similar habitats; grassland and forested areas.

Australopithecus afarensis, a *hominin* that lived 3.85 - 2.95 million years ago. Found in Eastern Africa, this species is thought to be a direct or close relative of the lineage leading to *Homo sapiens.* The skull and brain are small, about the size of a chimpanzee, about 400 cm3. They were mostly bipedal and found in the African savannas and arboreal environments. They likely expanded their diet to include meat most likely from scavenging.

In 1974, in what is now Ethiopia, there was a remarkable find of several hundred pieces of bone representing about 40 percent of a female skeleton, and this specimen was given the scientific name, *Australopithecus afarensis* and classified as a member of the tribe *Hominin*, a taxonomic rank between family and genus.

Estimated to have lived 3.2 million years ago she was given the common name **Lucy**, after the Beatles' song *Lucy in the Sky with Diamonds* which was played often by the anthropologists on that dig. She measured 3 ½ feet tall and weighed 60-65 pounds. The skeleton indicates evidence of Lucy being bipedal, walking on two legs. This is evidence that bipedalism preceded increase in brain size. In 2013, Ethiopia expressed a desire to bring Lucy back. She now resides at the National Museum of Ethiopia in Addis Ababa.

Australopithecus africanus (not to be confused with *afarensis*) roamed southern Africa between 3.3-2.1 million years ago and is thought also to be in the lineage leading to modern humans. It is anatomically similar to *A. afarensis*, with a combination of human-like and ape-like features. It had long arms and sloping face, a slender build and a pelvis built for slightly better bipedalism than that of *A. afarensis*. It appeared to be a bit more similar to modern humans. The brain size ranged from 420 - 500 cm3

Australopithecus sediba fossil remains date to about 2 million years ago and is also likely on the direct lineage to modern humans. The brain has a volume of 420 cm3 and their height was about 4'3". Its morphology suggests that this species may have been transitional between *A. africanus* and either *Homo habilis* or *Homo erectus*.

At the time of the last glacial age, 2.6 million years ago, well after the divergence of humanoids from chimpanzees, a gene which is associated with brain cell growth, was mutated to an alter form. This altered gene, SRGAP2 helped our brain cells grow faster and make more connections – enabling the brain to become more complex, a significant event in the evolution of *Hominins*.

The researchers acknowledged that they failed to prove the species is the direct ancestor of humankind. "The jury is out on the claim that it is an ancestor of the kind that gave rise to the genus *Homo*," which includes modern humankind, said Rick Potts, director of the human-origins program at the Smithsonian National Museum of Natural History in Washington. *"It is such an amalgam: It climbed trees, walked on the ground, likely used tools and might have been a dead end."*

Homo habilis or "Handy Man" was so named because of evidence of tools found with its remains, evidence of stone tool usage. He was discovered in eastern Africa and lived between 2.33 and 1.4 million years ago at a time of global cooling that produced large grasslands. This species still retained some ape-like morphology, its arms nearly as long as its legs. It weighed about 70 pounds and was about 50 inches tall, with a brain size about 600 cm3, about half that of modern humans. *H. habilis* seemed to lack hunting skill and relied upon scavenging recently killed large mammals, as animal bones uncovered showed carnivore marks as well as man-made marks indicating the use of primitive stone tools to dismember the previously killed animals. There was evidence that tools were also used to crush the bones for their marrow. *H. habilis* may have been the prey of sabre-tooth cats which roamed Africa 5 million to1.2 million years ago.

Homo ergaster commonly called *Workman*, from the Greek, as large stone tools were found associated with the fossils. This species was the first of our ancestors to look more like modern humans. They roamed Eastern and Southern Africa 1.8 - 1.3 million years ago. Unlike earlier species, their legs were much longer than the arms, so the limb proportions were similar to those of modern humans. Tree climbing adaptations of earlier species had been lost and had given way to a long-legged striding walk that was an efficient way to move about and made it easier to travel longer distances.

Females grew to about 62 inches and males reached 70 inches with a brain size of about 860 cm3. Their body may have been relatively hairless as a way of improving body cooling by sweating. *H. egaster* may have been the first to have a human-like voice, to harness fire, whether by obtaining it from natural occurrences or by igniting artificial fire. Their tools were mainly used on meat, bone, animal hides and wood. There is no archaeological evidence that *H. ergaster* had symbolic thought such as figurative art or buried their dead. Fossils found in Eurasia in the Republic of Georgia may represent the earliest evidence for the emergence of early humans from Africa into Eurasia 1.75 million years ago. *Homo ergaster* is considered to be the common ancestor of two groups of humans that took different evolutionary paths. One of these groups was *Homo erectus*, the other group ultimately became our own species *Homo sapiens.*

Homo erectus "Upright Man". The earliest fossil relics date to about 1.8 million years ago and the most recent date to around 143,000 years ago. It originated in Africa but spread out to western and mid-Europe, India, China and Java starting about 1.75 million years ago. The "Java Man" fossil was first discovered in East Java, Indonesia in 1891 and dated to about 1.66 million years. This would suggest that *H. erectus* spanned a period of about a million years and spread over a large habitat range. Fossils discovered vary and as such there are still ongoing debates as to the scientific classification of this species. Adults were slender, and weighed between 90 to 150 lbs. They stood slightly over five feet to nearly six foot; evidence of a large variation of skeletal size variation. Brain size varied over its habitat range and chronology. The earliest remains show a cranial capacity of 850 cm^3, about 60% of today's typical brain while the latest Javan specimens measure up to 1100 cm^3. This is evidence for selection leading towards increased encephalization.

The stone tools they manufactured were used as a scraping or cutting tool or possibly they could have been used in hand to hand combat, or tossed at foe or prey. It has been suggested that *H. erectus* may have been the first hominid to use rafts to travel over oceans.

Their disappearance in Asia, may have been caused by the Toba Super-eruption in Indonesia 69,000 to 77,000 years ago. This volcanic eruption caused a world wide volcanic winter lasting 6-10 years. A recently published article in the journal *Nature* 448, 201-204, August 08, 2012, titled: *New fossils from Koobi Fora in northern Kenya confirm taxonomic diversity in early Homo*, present evidence of two contemporary species of *Homo erectus. The* newly discovered *Homo* species fossils, have been dated to between 1.78 and 1.95 million years old. These two, still not given scientific names, from Eastern Africa, were contemporaries geographically and temporally with *Homo erectus*, which is our direct ancestor.

Homo antecessor, discovered in Spain, dates to 1.2 million to 800,000 years ago. Rather tall, 5 1/2 to 6 feet and weighed about 200 pounds, however their brain was slightly smaller than modern man, about 1,100 cm3. Fossil and tools remains have also been discovered in England, dating to 950,000 years ago, making *H. antecessor* the earliest genus *Homo* in Northern Europe.

Homo heidelbergensis was first discovered near Heidelberg, Germany in 1907. It appears intermediate between *Homo erectus* and fully modern humans. They originated between 800,000 and 1,300,000 years ago, and continued until about 200,000. It ranged over east and south Africa, Europe and west Asia. One theory is that *H. sapiens* probably evolved from *H. heildelbergensis* between 200,000 and 100,000 years ago in Africa, and the European branch evolved towards Neanderthals some 300,000 years ago in Europe. Another theory is that *Homo sapiens*' ancestor was *H. antecessor*. The debate continues.

H. heidelbergensis had a large brain-case with a typical cranial volume of 1100–1400 cm3 overlapping the 1350 cm3 average of modern humans. They also had advanced tools and behavior. Males averaged about 5 ft 9 in. tall and 136 lbs. Females averaged 5 ft 2 in. and 112 lbs.

Homo neanderthalensis

Neanderthals is their common name and are often thought of as our brutish, dimwitted ancestors that lived in caves. They did occupy caves at times, they were stronger than us, but they may not have been all that dimwitted. However they are not our ancestors. *Homo neanderthalensis* was discovered in 1856 in the Neander Valley in Germany. http://www.nature.com/nature/journal/vaop/ncurrent/full/nature12788.html

They lived in a time of cooling climate, which would account for their robust physical stature. Neanderthals were more robust and stronger than *Homo sapiens*. Males stood about 5'6" weighing about 170-185 lbs. and females about 5' tall and weight about 145 lbs.

The lineages leading to modern humans and Neanderthals likely diverged in Africa between 500,000 - 700,000 years ago from a common ancestor, most likely, *Homo heidelbergensis*. This common ancestor later split into two parallel branches, one remaining in Africa until about 100,000 years ago and eventually producing modern man, *Homo sapiens*. The other branch migrated out of Africa to Europe and beyond. This branch later split again into two lineages about 300,000 years ago, Neanderthals and Denisovans. The Denisovans, classified as a sub species of *Homo sapiens,* are known from the DNA of a 80,000 year old bone fragment discovered in a cave called Denisova cave located in the Altai Mountains of Siberia, Russia. Douglas Quenqua, NYTimes, December 9, 2013. Neanderthal sites have been found throughout Europe from the Strait of Gibraltar, throughout Greece, Iraq, Russia to Mongolia.

An analysis conducted by Professors Eiluned Pearce and Robin Dunbar at the University of Oxford and Professor Chris Stringer at the Natural History Museum, London, as reported in *Science News,* March 19, 2013, indicates that Neanderthals' brains were similar in size to modern man's. Fossil data suggests, however, that their brain structure was rather different. The results show that larger areas of the Neanderthal brain, compared to the modern human brain, were given over to vision and movement, probably as a consequence of living in northern clines. This left less room for the higher level thinking required to form large social groups and for extensive creativity. Neanderthals were an advanced species, capable of intelligent thought processes and were able to adapt to and survive in some of the harshest environments known to humans. They were advanced tool makers, used fire, made and used clothing and lived in large complex social groups and occupied caves. Their diet consisted of both large animals and vegetation and, interesting enough, they buried their dead and occasionally marked grave sites. We would consider that Neanderthals had a rather sophisticated behavior.

Neanderthals and *Homo sapiens* likely shared some elements of speech and language. In the journal *Frontiers in Language Sciences*, July 2013, authors Dediu and Levinson argue that recognizably modern language is likely an ancient feature of our genus predating at least the common ancestor of both modern humans and Neanderthals. Thus, a period about a million years ago was the beginning of modern language.

A complete Neanderthal mitochondrial genome has been sequenced and analyzed. Some genetic studies have suggested that Neanderthals may have had red hair and light skin color and there may have been some interbreeding with *Homo sapiens*. However, there is ongoing rigorous debate whether Neanderthals and *Homo sapiens* did interbreed. When scientists discovered a few years ago that modern humans shared some genetic sequences of DNA with Neanderthals, their best explanation was that at some point the two species must have interbred. Scientists of the Neanderthal Genome Sequencing consortium suggest that interbreeding may have occurred when modern humans carrying Upper Paleolithic technologies encountered Neanderthals as they expanded out of Africa, most likely 47,000–65,000 years ago. http://www.plos.org DOI: 10.1371/journal.pgen.1002947, October 4, 2012.

Another detailed comparison of the Denisovan, Neanderthal, and human genomes has revealed evidence for a complex web of interbreeding among the lineages. Elizabeth Pennisi, Science 340: 799. 17 May 2013. However, yet another study by scientists at the University of Cambridge has questioned this conclusion, hypothesizing instead that the DNA overlap is a remnant of a common ancestor of both Neanderthals and modern humans. Anders Eriksson and Andrea Manica, http://www.pnas.org/content/109/35/13956. What can be concluded is that the lineages and interactions of the various Hominins remains complicated and is not yet completely resolved.

A recent discovery at the site of La Chapelle-aux-Saints cave, bordering the Sourdoire Valley, France, suggests the possibility that these evolutionary relatives of ours intentionally buried their dead, at least 50,000 years ago, before the arrival of anatomically modern humans in Europe. These discoveries support the contention that these Western European Neanderthals possessed complex symbolic behavior. PNAS, December 12, 2013.

A photo of a reconstructed Neanderthal along with an interesting article on *Last of the Neanderthals* can be found in National Geographic. http://ngm.nationalgeographic.com/2008/10/neanderthals/hall-text/1 Here they report on an extensive cave system called El Sidrón, discovered in Northern Spain. The cave had the fossilized remains of a group of Neanderthals who lived and perhaps died violently, approximately 43,000 years ago. The bones had cut marks that were made by the blow of a stone tool. The inference is that these Neanderthals were cannibalized for their bone marrow and brains. The reason could have been ritual or starvation or they could have become victims. In another Neanderthal cave, farther south on the Rock of Gibraltar, researchers discovered stone spearpoints and scrapers. This cave was occupied from 125,000 years ago until their disappearance 28,000 years ago. Neanderthals occupied a large range and their disappearance occurred in pockets at different locations and different times, which coincided with climatic changes as well as the appearance of *Homo sapiens*. Gibraltar is certainly one of their last outposts.

The many factors suggested for Neanderthals demise include their lack of fitness to the warming environment and the organization of their brain which may have lessened their social, competitive and creative skills. What is certain is that there was overlap with *Homo sapiens* and other *hominins* both temporally and geographically. These *hominins* most likely hunted the same animals for food. There is a postulate in evolutionary theory that states no two non-interbreeding species can occupy the same niche. Niche is the way of life of a species; the sum of the habitat requirements that allow a species to persist and produce off-spring. If two non-interbreeding species occupy the same territory and depend the same foods and resources, that is they occupy the same niche, one will replace the other. Did *Homo sapiens* witness this extinction of Neanderthals? Or did they participate in their extinction?

3

Homo Sapiens

"As evolutionary time is measured, we have only just turned up and have hardly had time to catch our breath, still marveling at our thumbs, still learning to use the brand-new gift of language. Being so young, we can be excused all sorts of folly and can permit ourselves the hope that someday, as a species, we will begin to grow up."
LEWIS THOMAS

I GATHERED THE names and brief characterizations of just a few of our ancestral primates in chronological order, to give a glimpse of our journey to modern man. This is certainly not meant to be a comprehensive nor definitive survey, merely a broad brushstroke to show that human evolution is quite real. This lineage is continuous without any important missing links and quite importantly, we humans are animals and have been given the scientific name, *Homo sapiens.* The history of man is still being written. Research is vigorous and ongoing.

What we do know is that about 1.8 million years ago, our early ancestors were living on the divide of forests and grasslands. Full bipedalism was not yet developed. They were of small stature and had small brains. By several hundred thousand years later these early African *hominins* had left the forests for the grasslands, developed larger brains, flatter faces and upright bodies better suited to walking. It was about this time that these *hominins* spread throughout Africa and into Eastern Europe, Asia and Indonesia. *Homo habilis, Homo erectus* and others developed traits suitable for these new environments. They became diverse morphologically in different localities. Scientists have discovered specimens in the same location and dating to the same time, but having variable morphological traits. As a consequence of these confusing finds, paleoanthropologists can be grouped into either splitters or lumpers.

Lumpers and Splitters, are terms used by taxonomists to characterize two groups of biologists that either group specimens having somewhat similar characteristics into one large diverse species, the *Lumpers*; as opposed to other biologists, the *Splitters*, that believe the same specimens represent more than one species. Paleoanthropologist are no exception.

Hence, there is controversy revolving around an acceptable definition of what exactly is a species. The simple and traditional definition of a species is a group of living organisms consisting of similar individuals capable of interbreeding and producing viable and fertile offspring. The horse and donkey's offspring, the viable but sterile mule is evidence that the parents are of two species. Dogs, with a large diversity of breeds, are of one species. Offsprings of the different breeds meet the criteria of one species, *Canis domesticus*. Unfortunately, the archeological tools available cannot determine the viability and fertility of any offspring that may have occurred between diverse hominins. What can be stated with certainty is that a more accurate accounting of the lineage leading to man will change as new discoveries and research continues. One can also confidently say that any change in this history of man will be in the minor details; that the present survey is reasonable accurate.

Incidentally, scientific binomial nomenclature, the use of the taxonomic system of genus and species, was developed by Carolus Linnaeus (1707 - 1778) a Swedish botanist, zoologist and physician, as a system for describing and ranking all organisms. The binomial nomenclature is still used today. Linnaeus is known as the father of taxonomy.

"It is disturbing to discover in oneself these curious revelations of the validity of the Darwinian theory. If it is true that we have sprung from the ape, there are occasions when my own spring appears not to have been very far."
CORNELIA OTIS SKINNER

We know that kids sometimes act like monkeys, but this usually refers to their energy levels and dexterity on playground monkey bars. To take a more serious examination of similarities of humans to lower animals, and to have a better understanding of the behavior of modern humankind, it may be well to have a brief look at the chimpanzees and compare their behavior to our own.

After early *hominins* split from chimpanzees five to seven million years ago, they progressed to live as hunter-gatherer tribes consisting of many small bands of 30 or so people. Each band would have consisted of closely related individuals and that cooperation between members within the band provided a strong foundation for the view that cooperative behavior, as distinct from the fierce aggression as observed between chimp groups, was their norm.

The similarity of DNA between humans and chimpanzees has been estimated to be between 95% to 98.5% depending on which nucleotides are counted and which are excluded. June 2013, *Science Now*. In other words, with respect to our shared DNA, we are very close to the apes.

Dr. Jane Goodall, a British primatologist is best known for her 45-year study of social and family interactions of wild chimpanzees in Gombe Stream National Park in Tanzania. She observed behaviors such as hugs, kisses, tickling, self-awareness and self-interest, pats on the back, and grief, traits that we would consider human.

Chimpanzees live in male hierarchical social groups which can range from 40-60 individuals and occasionally, individuals would switch from one group to another. Switching may add to a communities genetic diversity. Members of these groups develop strong affectionate bonds with each other that can last a lifetime. Mother daughter bonds are very strong. Bonding has also been observed between siblings and pairs of males.

A chimp community is organized more or less in linear fashion. It establishes social standing, with one male at the top, the "alpha" position dominating all females, although females have their own hierarchy, albeit much less straightforward. Disputes within the group are often handled with gestures and posturing rather than actual attacks.

However, Chimps are capable of physical violence between tribes. Dr. Goodall observed a 4 years territory war between two groups of chimps that ended with one group killing all the other chimps in the other group.

Regardless of the exact percentage, most evolutionists believe that humans and apes share a common ancestor. We, *Homo sapiens,* originated in Africa, and obtained our anatomical modernity 200,000 years ago and began to exhibit full behavioral modernity around 50,000 years ago. While other *hominins* migrated out of Africa 1.75 million years ago, *H. sapiens* migrated out of Africa about 70,000 years ago. We were hunter-gatherers until about 10,000 years ago.

One need not be apologetic nor ashamed that we are indeed animals and that we have a scientific name. We all are animals. The acceptance of the reality that we are animals may, for some, be difficult. However there is not a legitimate reason to deny these facts. With this realization, we can have a perspective about humans unclouded by mysticism, folklore or fanciful thinking. Perhaps this is a different perspective; but there are repercussions we should all be aware of, for the common good of humanity.

In a nod to the CBS television series, Survivor. *Homo sapiens* outwitted, outplayed and outlasted all other species in our genus.

For those that would enjoy a wider view of human evolution, Lone Survivors; How We Came to be the Only Humans on Earth, by paleoanthropologist Chris Stringer would be an excellent choice.

4

We Are Unique

"Behavior is what man does, not what he thinks, feels or believes."
EMILY DICKINSON

Human Traits

THERE ARE NUMEROUS human traits, some of which I find disturbing and others which may assist in sustaining life into the future. I have been selective, not inclusive and have chosen those traits which may be significant in this critique of *Homo sapiens*. Our traits may be hard wired, that is inherited, however our traits do work within the framework of our accumulated knowledge and our environment.

There are man-made crises that face humanity; over population, the climate crisis, and the disparity of wealth that came about by man, without thought of the long term consequences. In a sense, they just happened, as humans were acting just as one would expect humans to act.

Sometimes we act instinctively, sometimes only after considered thought. Regardless, actions occurs only after brain activity, within the brain that we inherited from our ancestors. However many of our traits and behaviors are identical or similar to our ancestors. We have developed a high level of creativity, insight, imagination, sense of humor, intelligence, empathy, compassion, love and self-awareness. Least we forget, we humans are also capable of disgraceful and disgusting behavior.

There are some 200 human traits that most agree are genetically determined. Handedness, free or attached earlobes, eye color, hair color, straight or curly hair, sexual orientation, allergies, schizophrenia and colorblindness are just a few of the physical genetic traits. We also have behavioral traits, such as love, compassion, fear, rage and our tendency to gather as groups that have cultural similarities.

All behavioral traits are coded within our DNA in the cells of our brain, and hence are hardwired and are inherited from our ancestors. All behaviors are expressed by a complex interaction of the chemicals such as neurotransmitters and hormones and the structures, neuron, within the brain. The brain with its centralized control allows for rapid and coordinated responses to changes in the environment.

Which behaviors are learned or genetic, may not always be known with certainty. Outside influences certainly affect behavior, such as cultural values, ethics, authority and coercion. Scientists are finding genetic links to behavior and publishing their results in the scientific literature.

For convenience and clarity, *Behavior* is the way one acts or conducts oneself. *Trait* will be used as a distinguishing quality or characteristic which presumably has a genetic connection.

Certainly not all the human traits and behaviors will be covered herein. I have selected behaviors and traits that cause *Homo sapiens* to be both humane and inhumane.

"All things are subject to interpretation. Whichever interpretation prevails at a given time is a function of power and not truth."
FRIEDRICH NIETZSCHE

Regardless, if a certain behavior is learned or inherited, our perception is often warped.

Humans are very selective in their perceptions of the world. We have selective hearing, selective sight, selective memory. We know that children have selective hearing. Remember when your mother called out to you to wash up and come to dinner, just when you were in the middle of your favorite game. You continued playing. She calls again, this time she just says, "The pizza is ready." Within four seconds you are at the table, however you didn't stop to wash up. Adults are likewise selective. People with conservative leanings only watch Fox News and liberals listen to NPR. One would think that if humans were rational and intelligent that they would want to learn from both sides. This rarely happens.

Our vision is selective as well. We drive along the road really only seeing what is important for safe driving. The color of the cars around us are unnoticed. We to pay attention to only what we deem important. We are oblivious to the rest of the world unless there is an immediate and unexpected change in our world. "I saw it with my own eyes. I know what I saw", spoken as if one's perception of the world is as accurate as a camera. Unfortunately we have selective perception.

Another example; there are multiple witnesses to a bank robbery. There are multiple different accounts from the witnesses as to the description of the robber. There is false memory when we "remember" what didn't occur. The human brain is not as perfect as we may believe. All the sensory signals we receive are processed within our brain and are subject to the physical and chemical processes of the brain along with our prior memories.

What we all do have in common is that we are all *Homo sapiens*, one of millions of species of organism that have inhabited this planet. We certainly display a wide variety of behaviors. I think it is fascinating to examine some of these behaviors, from the perspective that we are *Homo sapiens*; and to question which component, nurture or nature guides our behavior. We do make decisions based upon the chemistry and structure of our brain and our stored memory. We have an evolutionary history that cannot be ignored. Our brain has evolved over hundreds of millions of years. Remember Pavlov's dog? The bell would ring. The dog salivated. Somehow that bell triggered the secretion of saliva. He certainly didn't think it through. Or, if a guy sees a pretty girl........ You know the rest of that story.

Identifying the origins of any trait may be difficult. However we do know that certain regions and chemicals within our brain play a role in our behaviors. Having a bias is human. Prejudice is intellectually wrong; it's judgments without evidence. Our bias's are shaped by experiences, knowledge and one's genetic heritage. If your perception of your experiences, that which really was there in your environment, is "manipulated" by your brain, would not the decisions of our politicians and religious leaders likewise be just as distorted by their brain's selective processes? The decisions humans make as a result of the brain's "distorted" processing can have substantial consequences for themselves and for the rest of humanity.

Primer on the Human Brain

> *"The brain is more than an assemblage of autonomous modules, each crucial for a specific mental function. Every one of these functionally specialized areas must interact with dozens or hundreds of others, their total integration creating something like a vastly complicated orchestra with thousands of instruments, an orchestra that conducts itself, with an ever-changing score and repertoire."*
>
> OLIVER SACKS

The adult human brain weighs about 3 lbs. with a volume of around 1130 cm3 in women and 1260 cm3 in men; about 3.5 times larger than the ape's brain. The human brain contains about 86 billion neurons. Each neuron forms about 1,000 connections with other neurons; which totals 86 trillion connections; that is 86,000,000,000,000 connections. By comparison, a cockroach has about one million neurons while the chimpanzee has about 6.7 billion neurons. Over our evolutionary history, our brain has become larger due to the expansion of the cerebral cortex, especially the prefrontal cortex and the visual cortex responsible for processing visual information.

The Cerebral Cortex is the outermost layered structure of neural tissue of the cerebrum (brain). The cerebrum is divided into two cortices; the left and right hemispheres. The cerebral cortex is divided into four functional areas or lobes.

The *frontal lobe* is the forepart of the brain running from the forehead to the temples. The frontal lobe is associated with attention, abstract thinking, behavior, problem solving tasks, and physical reactions and personality. The *orbitofrontal cortex* region of the frontal lobe is involved in sensory integration, analyzing reward and punishment and thus critical for adaptive learning and is associated with compulsive and repetitive behavior. During human evolution the frontal lobe's expansion is linked to the our intellectual advancement.

The *parietal lobe* contains areas involved in somatosensation (touch, temperature and body position) hearing, language, attention, and spatial cognition.

Temporal lobes are involved in the retention of visual memories, processing sensory input, comprehending language, storing new memories, emotion, and deriving meaning.

Occipital lobe's main functions are visual reception, visual-spatial processing, movement, and color recognition.

Evolutionary biology and neuroscience studies suggest that *hominin* symbolic communicative capabilities co-evolved with the brain, resulting in some parts of the brain becoming proportionally larger. Humans have a larger prefrontal cortex than other primates and this probably enabled some of the neural connections necessary for generating abstract symbolic concepts and planning tasks. The evolution of human complex functional neural organization may have been a long-term process, involving at least a million years. Terrance Deacon, PNAS, 9000-9006, 2010.

There is also the view that modern neural organization is the result of a relatively sudden genetic mutation that took place in populations from Africa only 50,000 years ago. Klein & Edgar, The Dawn of Human Culture, 2002.

We start as a fertilized egg containing DNA from each of our parents, and here we are as mature adults with amazing behaviors. That pathway from our DNA to our social behavior is certainly complex and convoluted. Our genes are expressed either singularly or in concert with other genes coding for neurological networks, multiple transmitters and receptors and with our stored memory. All this interacts with our socialization and the environment we find ourselves, and we react, accordingly.

Our brain has developed high levels of abstract reasoning, language, problem solving and culture through social learning. We have developed intellectually with the advancement of science, art and the humanities. We have created complex music and great literature. The world of art is an expression of our brains. Technologically we are most wonderful. Our understanding of the universe, of physics and chemistry is at a level incomprehensible to most.

NASA's Voyager 1, launched in 1977, has finally reached interstellar space; the first time a spacecraft has been in the space between the stars; a distance three times the distance as Pluto. We have left our solar system and we are heading for the stars.

We appreciate fine dining and we wear designer clothing. We have color TV's, fancy cars, fats, proteins and carbohydrates in abundance. We have developed agriculture to a "fine art" - It's called Industrial Agriculture, Agribusiness or just Factory Farms. Meat is produced in enormous quantities on wide open ranges, feed lots and slaughter houses. We use genetically modified seeds and pesticides to increase crop production. You probably do not want to read the "Pig to Supermarket" story. We have plentiful food, well maybe for only half of us. We have yachts, OK, only the upper 1%, and 12 of us have walked on the moon. We have spread out over the entire planet and we seem to have overpopulated this planet as well. We are the species with, at times, great compassion and brilliance and we are the species that, at times, are capable of great brutality. We are the survivors: *Homo sapiens.*

The Amygdala

The amygdala, part of the limbic system, is a small almond shaped group of nuclei deep within the brain, within the medial temporal lobes. The amygdala plays a primary role in our procession of memory and emotional reactions such as fear, loathing and "love" and long term memory. In humans, when the brain receives a sensory stimulus indicating an imminent danger, the signal is routed first to the thalamus. From there, the information is sent out over two parallel pathways: the "short route" and the "long route". The short route, as previously described, conveys a fast, rough impression of the situation, because it is a sub-cortical pathway in which no cognition is involved. This pathway activates the amygdala which, through its central nucleus, generates emotional responses before any perceptual integration has even occurred and before the mind can form a complete representation of the stimulus.

However, information that has travelled by way of the long route is processed in the cortex and then on to the amygdala where, in conjunction with various levels of the cortical processing system, it is analyzed to determine the severity of the threat. This elaborate representation of the object is then compared with the contents of explicit memory, memory which is recalled automatically and which involves the subject's conscious recollection of things and facts. Remembrance of that past "dangerous stimulus" is stored in memory. Fear conditioning is a behavioral example in which organisms learn to predict aversive events. We can respond appropriately when a similar dangerous stimulus occurs in a similar situation. Pavlov's dog learned to associate a bell sound with the presentation of food and would salivate even when a bell was sounded without the presence of food. Joseph LeDoux, *The Emotional Brain, Fear and the Amygdala,* Cellular and Molecular Neurobiology, Vol. 23, October 2003. Additionally, the amygdala is important for learning as suggested by studies showing that experimental inactivation of the amygdala during learning prevents learning from taking place.

Fearful actions or events get our full attention, yet fear is a very useful and well used tool of political operatives; recall those 30 second TV ads, produced by Madison Avenue for politicians. We despise them. Ever wonder why these *"scare the living daylights out of you"* ads show up on TV? It's most obvious; they are very effective. We easily recall ads telling us, with accompanying gruesome video that voting for the other fellow will reduce the earth to a pile of ashes. They have such great impact that the memory of these ads are stored in our long-term memory. Would it not be most wonderful if candidates for political office would simply state *their* qualifications, *their* agenda and pledge to not profit from the office? Of course, no savvy candidate would commit to this. So, I fear, we will continue to see those TV ads trying to scare us to death. I really loathe them.

Memory

"There are lots of people who mistake their imagination for their memory"
JOSH BILLINGS

Human brains are of sufficient size to store decades of memories with sufficient storage space for future memories. There is not a specific location in the brain that is the memory center. The memory process is brain-wide; a complex web of neurons spreads across relevant cortices. Our senses receive signals which are encoded and transmitted to the appropriate areas of the brain: the frontal, parietal, temporal and or occipital lobes, as appropriate.

When we observe a particularly beautiful flower, we look and smell the flower, feel the summer's breeze and hear birds chirping. Various appropriate areas of the brain receive encoded messages. We consolidate new related experiences with older experiences, such as related encoded experiences of the flowers of a previous Springtime outing. What seems to be a single memory is a complex construction. Recalling a memory effectively reactivates the neural patterns generated during the original encoding. Short term and long term memories are encoded and stored in different ways and in different parts of the brain. http://www.scientificamerican.com/article.cfm?id=what-is-the-memory-capacity

False Memory

> *"The difference between false memories and true ones is the same as for jewels: it is always the false ones that look the most real, the most brilliant."*
>
> SALVADOR DALI

Why is "The Truth" so difficult to establish, especially relating to human recall? We send people to jail, even to death row based upon eye witness accounts and occasionally the verdict is overturned based upon DNA evidence. Is our memory tainted by the need for resolution, justice or revenge?

I find it interesting that people of religion have certainty concerning their religious convictions. Absolute certainty. Their convictions cannot be shaken, even when confronted with information that contradicts their beliefs. While thinking about the unshakable aspect of some of our memory, I started to think about the studies concerning false memory. There may be a connection.

We know from our own experience that our memory often fails, that it can have mistaken or false recollection. There are many factors that can act during witnessing, encoding and retrieval of the event which may adversely affect the creation and maintenance of that memory.

In an article titled: *Creating a False Memory in the Hippocampus*, published in Science, July 26, 2013, Vol. 341, scientists at the Riken-M.I.T. Center for Neural Circuit Genetics at the Massachusetts Institute of Technology have reported that they have created a false memory in a mouse and have provided detailed clues to how such memories may form in human brains. Scientists report that they caused mice to remember being shocked in one location, when in reality the electric shock was delivered in a completely different location. Physical traces of a specific memory can be identified in a group of brain cells as it forms, and activated later by stimulating the same cells. They identified and chemically labeled the cells in the animals' brains where that memory was being formed; a rather simple experiment to locate in the brain areas responsible for memory.

Dr. Tonegawa, a lead scientist in this study said that because the mechanisms of memory formation are almost certainly similar in mice and humans, part of the importance of the research is *"to make people realize even more than before how unreliable human memory is,"* particularly in criminal cases when so much is at stake.

Dr. Elizabeth F. Loftus, a cognitive psychologist at University of California, Irvine, is an expert on human memory. Loftus is best known for her groundbreaking work on the misinformation effect and eyewitness memory and the creation and nature of false memories, including recovered memories of childhood sexual abuse. She has conducted extensive research on the malleability of human memory; that it is susceptible to misinformation and that our ability to recall events, our eye witness account may be flawed, concluding that our memory is volatile. In a laboratory study, she has found that 25% of subjects came to develop a "memory" for the event which had never taken place. Dr. Loftus has testified and advised courts about the nature of eyewitness memory for many cases including the McMartin preschool trial, O.J. Simpson, Ted Bundy, the trial of Oliver North, the officers accused in the Rodney King beating and the trial of the Menendez brothers.

It has long been speculated that mistaken eyewitness identification plays a major role in the wrongful convictions of innocent individuals. Mistaken eyewitness identification is responsible for more convictions of the innocent than all other factors combined. *The Innocence Project* determined that 75% of the 239 DNA exoneration cases had occurred due to inaccurate eyewitness testimony.

Incidentally, in November 18, 2010, The Bronowski Art&Science Forum featured as co-presenters Professor Loftus and Artist Deborah Aschheim in a forum entitled "Lest We Forget - Memory".

Nature versus Nurture

> *"Nature's patterns sometimes reflect two intertwined features: fundamental physical laws and environmental influences. It's nature's version of nature versus nurture."*
> BRIAN GREENE

We know that some of our human behavioral traits are inherited genetically from our ancestor's DNA and that some behaviors are cultural, that is learned; traits passed down from one generation to the next through a sort of schooling. The nurture constituent would include the language we speak, our religious and political preferences; these are not genetically based as such. Other traits that reflect our underlying talents and temperaments such as complex symbolic thinking, how proficient with language a person is, how religious, how liberal or conservative—are partially heritable.

"*Nature is all that a man brings with himself into the world; nurture is every influence that affects him after his birth.*" Francis Galton (1822 – 1911) and cousin of Charles Darwin. Galton, the English Victorian polymath first coined the phrase "Nature versus Nurture" as used in its modern sense. Two centuries earlier, the viewpoint that humans acquire all or almost all their behavioral traits from nurture was termed *tabula rasa* ("blank slate") by John Locke, (1632 – 1704), an English philosopher and physician.

Some individuals display hatred towards others that is deplorable. Our leaders decide to wage war using a cost to benefit ratio formula. Their decisions are rational; other times, irrational. At times we remember with clarity; other times we remember what we want to remember. We certainly have empathy of those less fortunate. Some individuals embrace compassion and charity. Some humans have behaviors that the rest of us would deem despicable.

We vote Republican or we vote Democratic because; well just because. We believe we remember every event exactly as it occurred, but we are sure others have faulty or selective memory. Some of us have uncontrolled anger, which carries on for some time. Some of us are rational and objective. Others are rash, irresponsible and harbor resentment or hatred. Some individuals display odd or dysfunctional behavior and behave badly while others are the positive contributors to our civilization. There are crooks, scammers and schemers amongst us. Others are artists, poets, musicians, scientists, innovators and philanthropists and just ordinary good people. We are certainly an odd bunch.

To better understand the nature-nurture conundrum, the relative contribution of our genes and our environment affecting our behavior, *The Minnesota Twin* studies are helpful. These twin studies, started in 1989 and were conducted at The University of Minnesota Center for Twin and Family Research, https://mctfr.psych.umn.edu. Researchers studied 1,400 pairs of identical and same-sex fraternal twins and their families. They discovered that identical twins reared apart are far more similar in personality than randomly selected pairs of people. Likewise, identical twins are more similar than fraternal twins. Also, biological siblings are more similar in personality than adoptive siblings. In another study conducted by Thomas Bouchard, et.al. and published in the Journal, Science, *250*, p. 223-228, the researchers found that on multiple measures of personality, temperament, occupational and leisure-time interests, and social attitudes, monozygotic twins reared apart are about as similar as are monozygotic twins raised together. These studies suggest that our behavior, our personality is to some degree, genetically determined.

Sexual attraction is certainly a genetic trait originating millions of years ago. Heterosexual human males often (sometimes) will notice and look at young females with large breasts. Even some married males look while in the presence of their spouses, but do so without moving their heads. Do dads teach their sons to ogle females? I think it comes naturally.

Then there are those politicians and religious leaders that preach high moral standards, but are unable to keep their penises in their pants knowing full well that if they are caught in such behavior their career will be greatly tarnished or destroyed. What were they thinking?

> *"God gave men both a penis and a brain, but unfortunately not enough blood supply to run both at the same time."*
> ROBIN WILLIAMS, COMMENTING ON THE CLINTON/LEWINSKY AFFAIR

What we do or at least should learn from our dads and moms is to be respectful. Genetically speaking, males sneak a peek. In one sense, males learn that females are not sex symbols; or are they? Advertisers are keenly aware. Without the biological drive to reproduce, where would we be?

Why do many boys play games with violent overtones such as cops and robbers, Cowboys and Indians and some of the video games? They consider these games as fun. Perhaps they learn from older boys. Could it be genetic? Young girls play nurturing games often with their dolls. Do they learn this from their mothers? What about the story *Lord of the Flies* by William Golding? It's the story of young boys isolated on an island and how they handle difficult situations. It's a fictional story, but its resonates.

So the question: is it nurture, how we are brought up, our parenting, our friends, our environment that makes us what we are, or is it just in our genes?

As we now know, both genetics and the environment interact in the development and behavior of *Homo sapiens*; a simple debate is quite meaningless.

We are Tribal

Early humans moved out from the rainforests and onto the grasslands of Africa where there were game animals to hunt and tubers and other high carbohydrate foods could be found; sort of a Garden of Eden existence. Hunting-gathering was reasonably successful and this led to an increase of their populations. As weapons became more sophisticated and man more mobile and cunning, early humans having greater high value food sources survived and procreated. Presumedly, as tribes became large and perhaps a bit unruly, groups split off to form new tribes. Inter and intra tribal competition likely occurred. When resources were difficult to secure, warfare likely started between similar tribes and perhaps between *Homo sapiens* and other closely related species of *hominins*. There seems to have been overlap geographically and temporally with other species that occupied the same niche. The strong tribes defeated the weaker ones, as a matter of survival. We don't know what happened of course, just reasonable conjecture. Competition might have led to migration out of Africa and eventually the whole world.

Tribal existence provided the hub for learning and passing on tracking and hunting skills; knowledge of the prey's habits and techniques to kill the prey. The skills of the gatherers, identifying the habitat of the edible plants, were tribal essentials. It is likely the elderly assisted in raising and teaching the young. The tribe was where everyone slept and fed together; safety in numbers. This close proximity of individuals may have given rise to the very human trait of empathy, identifying with the pain of another individual. Chimpanzees exhibit grooming and comforting behavior towards others. Soothing may be an appropriate description. This behavior may be an incipient form of empathy, identifying with another individual's situation; of feeling another's pain. The ability or insight to recognize the pain or discomfort of others may have been what made *Homo sapiens* what we identify as human.

Tribal benefits include greater opportunities for mating, grooming, heat conservation and food. A species that is instinctively kind to their own tribe members and could judge the moral character of others, has an evolutionary advantage. The altruistic nature of tribal animals is comprehensible when considering the benefits of sharing goods and services. Non-sharing individuals stand alone. Our basic morality may have been one factor, a factor that seems to be genetically determined, passed on through our genes from one generation to the next. There are costs to individuals within a tribe. The chance of receiving parasites or other pathogens increases with the number of members as does intra-tribal conflict and reproductive competition.

Dunbar's number, proposed by British anthropologist Robin Dunbar is a calculated optimal tribal size of early humans. The bases of this calculation is the relationship of primate brain size with their tribal size and then extrapolating to early *Homo sapiens*. He proposed that humans can only comfortably maintain 150 stable relationships. Tribes larger than this generally require larger long-term memory, more restrictive rules, laws, and enforced norms to maintain a stable, cohesive group. As groups increased in group size, splintering would likely occur.

Cooperation is instinctual and was a major factor in the survival of *Homo sapiens*, says Michael Tomasello, an American psychologist and Co-director of the Max Planck Institute for Evolutionary Anthropology in Leipzig, Germany. He has synthesized three decades of published research to develop a comprehensive evolutionary theory of human cooperation. The very early ancestors of humans were apes that occupied dense rainforests where food gathering was individual. Cooperation was not necessary for the apes. When early humans moved out onto the grasslands, they scavenged the carcasses of game animals that had previously been killed. This was the primary source of their protein. Our early ancestors were tribal and presumable developed cooperative behavioral instincts. As they developed hunting skills, organized group hunts would have been necessary to bring down large game. This intra-dependent collective behavior was the antecedent to the development of language and art. http://www.nytimes.com/2011/03/11/science/11kin.html

Charles Darwin, in his book *The Descent of Man*, a discourse on human evolution, covers societal issues concerning evolutionary theory, ethics, psychology, sexual selection as well as differences between human races. Darwin postulated that *Homo sapiens* succeeded because of their traits of compassion and sharing; traits that would benefit to the whole tribe. Wealth-sharing assured that the tribe survived.

Human's success as a species is in part because we were tribal animals.

Tribal is characterized as having a tendency to form groups, with strong group loyalty. We belong to various tribes: Republicans, Democrats or Libertarians, we support our favorite sports team, we are members of the Sierra Club, the PTA, the Rotary Club and any other numerous clubs and affiliations. We most likely belong to several tribes. We fly their colors. We have bumper stickers. We dress to fit with the fashion of our tribe. For some it might be designer outfits, for others, hiking apparel. For some it may be a wedge shaped cheese hat. We echo our tribe's sentiments: "No new taxes." "He's a faggot." "Capitalism is the best policy to insure lasting freedom and prosperity." "Protect the Polar Bears and the Rainforest." "Stop the Keystone XL Pipeline." *"Give Peace a Chance."* This last phrase; it's lovely, but we rarely practice peace; we seem to always be at war. The atrocities of war are horrendous.

Certain behaviors align themselves with either conservative values or liberal points of view. These tribal differences have led us into contentious situations. We can be extremely loyal. We seem not readily able to be skeptical or suspicious of the veracity of those 30 second political TV ads with very unflattering photos of the opposition, unless, of course, they are bashing the other side. We readily accept our side's message as truthful. When one is faced with a sticky question, such as, if you are against abortion, why do you favor the death penalty? The common response is *"I don't want to go there"*. When faced with a contradiction to one's belief, for some people there is a disconnect.

5

Good Traits and Behaviors

There are certain human traits and behaviors that I consider as good traits; those that contribute to the survival of humans long term. There are other traits and behaviors I shall label as bad traits; those that may be causative agents for a shortened period of human existence. Simply, good traits lead to the continuance of our species in relative comfort. Bad traits are those that may lead to our demise. While the terms good and bad are a bit naive, generalized and simplistic they will satisfy for the sake of this discussion. The division between good and bad may lead to debate, which I encourage.

Forward Vision-Imagination

When I was about 7 or 8 years of age, living in Monterey, Saturday afternoons were often spent at the movie theater. My friends and I would gather to see Western movies; black and white at the time. After the movie was over, we would saunter out of the theater and on to Alvarado Street, each of us emulating the ambling or strutting of the cowboys we just witnessed. We held our hands at our sides pretending to have our six shooters at the ready. We certainly had imagination. We were able to produce fanciful images in our brains embracing the heroic antics of our movie heroes.

When this trait in our evolutionary history occurred is unknown. The development surely increased as our brains increased in size. It would have happened gradually. Imagination and self awareness were probably an early form of cognition; the ability to plan and foresee the future. *"Where will the game animals be tomorrow? If I take a shortcut over to the watering hole, I'm sure they will show up a little later."* I surmise that the ability to anticipate future events, to be able to consider most all consequences is most important to the survival of *Homo sapiens.*

Scientists at the Department of Psychological and Brain Sciences, Dartmouth College, have published studies that suggest that conscious manipulation of mental representations is central to many creative and uniquely human abilities. Using functional Magnetic Resonance Imaging, (fMRI) on human subjects, scientists can measure brain activity by detecting associated changes in blood flow. Researchers revealed that a widespread neural network performs specific mental manipulations on the contents of visual imagery. Evidence for such a complex, interconnected network has been difficult to produce with current techniques that mainly study brain activity in isolation and are insensitive to distributed informational processes. They conclude that as of yet, "We do not know how the human brain mediates complex and creative behaviors such as artistic, scientific, and mathematical thought."

http://www.pnas.org/content/early/2013/09/13/1311149110

Compassion, Empathy, Hope, Love and the Human Spirit

> *"Love and compassion are necessities, not luxuries. Without them, humanity cannot survive."*
> DALAI LAMA XIV, THE ART OF HAPPINESS

Compassion amongst humans is common and we all consider that fortunate, but it's not all that common. We pass by a beggar, a vet obviously suffering from mental problems, a hitchhiker, all people in need. A few of us stop to assist; others keep on their journey. Words we associate with compassion include kind, considerate, understanding and humanitarian.

There is an interesting human activity: *Practice random acts of kindness.* There is a sense of warmth when practiced; it is sometimes infectious. In the odd chance you are not familiar with random acts of kindness, it is a selfless act performed by a person or people wishing to either assist or cheer up an individual or individuals. Also written as the phrase: *"Practice random kindness and senseless acts of beauty"* and is attributed to Anne Herbert.

We make decisions to whom we extend some compassion. It seems obvious that we can't help everyone; we can't hand out a few dollars to all that need it. If we did, we would be just as broke. Sometimes we are a bit afraid that the homeless person or the hitchhiker will rob us. Sometimes we wonder why they don't just get their act together and find a job. We rationalize that *they* will just spend it on booze or drugs. Sometimes we're heartless. How do we explain the *"pay it forward"* sensibility of some compassionate individuals some of the time? Are we more genetically inclined to show compassion or to walk on depending upon which genes were passed on down to us? Does our brain make instantaneous decisions as to when it is appropriate?

Pay it forward is an expression for describing the beneficiary of a good deed repaying it to others instead of to the original benefactor.

> *"I do not pretend to give such a deed; I only lend it to you. When you [...] meet with another honest Man in similar Distress, you must pay me by lending this Sum to him; enjoining him to discharge the Debt by a like operation, when he shall be able, and shall meet with another opportunity. I hope it may thus go thro' many hands, before it meets with a Knave that will stop its Progress. This is a trick of mine for doing a deal of good with a little money."*
>
> Benjamin Franklin in a letter to Benjamin Webb, April 25, 1784.

However compassion seems to be associated with one's status. Studies by Berkeley psychologists Paul Piff and Dacher Keltner have shown that individuals from the upper social class were less compassionate and behave more unethically than lower-class individuals. Individuals with greater wealth and education are worse at recognizing the emotions of others and less likely to pay attention to people they are interacting. They are more likely to be more self-focused. The less we have to rely on others, the less we may care about their feelings. PNAS, vol. 109 no. 11, March 13, 2012.

I think most all would agree that the compassionate individual is one to emulate and admire. We all are aware of compassionate acts done by people without a vested interest and we admire these individuals. Plato compared the human soul to a chariot: the intellect is the driver and the emotions are the horses. Life is a continual struggle to keep the emotions under control. There are individuals with contrarian views who have considered compassion with derision. Emmanuel Kant, (1724-1804), a German philosopher, saw it as a weak and misguided sentiment. He said of compassion: "*Such benevolence is called soft-heartedness and should not occur at all among human beings.*" Laboratories at numerous universities that have researched compassion suggest that this emotion is rational, functional, and adaptive—a view which has its origins in Darwin's 1872 book, *Expression of Emotion in Man and Animals.*

The Center for Compassion and Altruism Research and Education (CCARE), at Stanford University has a stated goal to examine mechanisms underlying altruistic giving, using established neuroeconomic techniques to determine the neural bases of compassion and altruism and the factors that influence altruistic behavior. Using fMRI of the brain they hope to identify specific areas of the brain that are related to the anticipation of pleasure and pain to gain a deep understanding of compassion and its associated human behaviors. An important stated aspect of CCARE is to critically engage with Buddhist and other contemplative traditions that contain a rich mental taxonomy and, what is more important, clearly delineate mental cultivation techniques aimed at developing and enhancing specific qualities of the human mind and heart. The results are presently unpublished.

http://neuroscience.stanford.edu/research/programs/program_info/CCARE_web.pdf

Empathy

> *"Education leads to enlightenment. Enlightenment opens the way to empathy. Empathy foreshadows reform."*
>
> Derrick A. Bell, Faces at the Bottom of the Well: The Permanence of Racism

Most humans have empathy; the ability to recognize, understand and share emotions that are being experienced by another. "I feel your pain".

After the Sandy Hook Elementary School shooting in Newtown, Connecticut, the outpouring of sympathy and gifts overwhelmed the township, leading city officials to plead to the public to not send any more gifts.

Empathy is an instinctive mirroring of other's experience. In the human brain, neural systems that are active when we are in pain, become engaged when we observe the suffering of others. When this trait of *Homo sapiens* arose is unknown. Using fMRI, scientists can visualize which part of the brain lights up, has intense electrical firing of nerve circuits and intense blood flow and oxygen consumption. As reported in Science Magazine, February 20, 2004, empathy has been shown to have a neurological basis. Researchers have found that the stronger you feel empathy for someone else's pain, the stronger the response in that part of your brain that is active when you are the recipient of pain. Our capacity to feel another's pain may explain why humans are not always selfish, but can exhibit altruistic and helpful behavior. When tragic events; school shootings, Boston bombings and the like are widely covered by television networks, there is "the identifiable victim effect."

Empathy is powerful. Psychopaths may lie, lack guilt and empathy seemingly from a disorder of their cognitive processing. The disadvantage of empathy is that it is parochial, it limits our worldview and we may, at certain times be better not to completely rely upon it. When television viewers have 24/7 coverage of a "stand your ground" event, humans identify with one or the other side; there is an identifiable victim. Empathy for the principles involved occupy our concerns, to the exclusion of other events; Wall Street financial problems, Senate filibusters, Sequestration, the Climate Crisis, starvation in undeveloped countries or even starvation amongst the poor in this country.

'Empathy is the latest code word for liberal activism, for treating the Constitution as malleable clay to be kneaded and molded in whatever form justices want. It represents an expansive view of the judiciary in which courts create policy that couldn't pass the legislative branch or, if it did, would generate voter backlash".

KARL ROVE

Politicians are clever, they pose with sickly or cute children rather than talk about their agenda. Religions rely on empathy, the suffering of their 'saints,' to garnish support from their followers. We humans have the amazing ability to focus our attention especially if we feel empathy. The National Resources Defense Council (NRDC) sends out donation requests with a photo of a sad eyed baby Polar Bear. However, the NRDC has an outstanding record in support of environmental issues. Their accomplishments occur when they file lawsuits against governmental agencies, such as the EPA to stop logging in primeval forest, stopping toxic dumping and sue the US Navy to stop the underwater sonic testing that causes damage to whales, dolphins and other oceanic organisms. The NRDC is clever; toxic dump sites are not enduring and create little empathy; that Polar Bear is rather cute. When deciding the significance of any event we face, it may be better to make analytical calculations rather than responding instantaneously with empathy.

Liking - Not Liking and Love

"Where in the brain is love located?", asked the artist, David Hockney of neuroscientists, Drs. Francis Crick and Tom Albright at the time of his visit to The Salk Institute in 1992.

Their response: "*The amygdala*".

What is Love? I'm not sure I could give a knowledgeable response, but we do know when we experience love. Liking, Loving and experiencing joy and probably disliking as well, seem similar in some ways. I would wager that the amygdala is involved in each of these experiences. With loving, our sex drive may be intertwined as well. Short and simplified, all these traits arose thousands or millions of years ago and have been inherited as coded DNA sequences. Not terribly romantic, but that's the story.

The Amygdala, small part of our brain that has a huge influence on our lives. Part of the limbic system it is a small almond shaped group of nuclei deep within the brain, within the medial temporal lobes that plays a primary role in our procession of memory and emotional reactions.

"Part of the reason men seem so much less loving than women is that men's behavior is measured with a feminine ruler".
FRANCESCA M. CANCIAN

Hope

"Man never made any material as resilient as the human spirit."
BERNARD WILLIAMS

Daniel A. Helminiak, a Catholic priest and theologian defines the human spirit as a function of the brain; it's an awareness, insight, understanding and judgment. It is doubtful that a specific location of the human brain could be identified as the human spirit loci, but the term is useful and widely used to explain a certain sort of hope that humans have or possess, "something" that we hold as worthy and is our better nature. Sometimes referred to as "*The Higher Component of Human Nature*". The Human Core of Spirituality: Mind as Psyche and Spirit, 1996.

"He that lives upon hope will die fasting"
BENJAMIN FRANKLIN

Recently, Billy Ray Cyrus appeared on the Piers Morgan TV show. The discussion centered on "Hope" and how important hope was in his life. He never wants to lose hope. There is a need for him to know that there is always hope. Hope for Billy Ray seems to be very essential for a meaningful life. Billy Ray had recently written and then performed a song about *Hope.* He is a very poetic song writer. Totally, there must be hundreds or thousands of songs that deal with hope. It is a prevalent human trait.

His concerns about hope reminded me that religions offer hope. Hope is the currency of religion. Hope, (from wikipedia) is the state which promotes the desire of positive outcomes related to events and circumstances in one's life or in the world at large. Hope and related emotions are a field of study in Psychology. Dr. Barbara L. Fredrickson, a Professor at the University of North Carolina, argues that Religious leaders are peddlers of hope. *"Hope comes into play when our circumstances are dire", when "things are not going well or at least there's considerable uncertainty about how things will turn out."* She states *"hope literally opens us up...[and] removes the blinders of fear and despair and allows us to see the big picture thus allowing us to become creative" and have "belief in a better future."* Psychology Today, March 23, 2009.

"Science is a very human form of knowledge"
JACOB BRONOWSKI

Can science *"remove the blinders of fear and despair and allow us to see the big picture?"* Science examines the Big Picture; it explains the how of the universe, not the why. Fear and despair arise often when we cannot comprehend events. Science offers an understanding based upon biological and physical principles. Science never offers hope. We can accept the findings of science, or ignore science and look elsewhere for explanations; religion is the usual alternative. Science does not offer hope, only explanations that withstand close scrutiny and are verifiable.

Morality

"The hottest places in hell are reserved for those who, in times of great moral crisis, maintain their neutrality."
DANTE ALIGHIERI, C. 1265–1321, INFERNO

Morality is a genetic trait passed through generations by way of our DNA. Surprised?

Researchers at the *Infant Cognition Center* at Yale University, Paul Bloom, Karen Wynn, Kiley Hamlin and other colleagues have published, in peer reviewed journals, some very interesting studies. In their laboratory, commonly called "The Baby Lab", scientists have observed that babies are born with a sense of morality. In unique studies, working with preverbal babies, some as young as 3 months and using puppets, the researchers have been able to quantify the preferences of these babies. Babies, too young to verbalize can fix their eyes on their preference or, babies a bit older, to reach out for their preference. Given the choice of good puppet and bad puppet acting out scenarios, babies chose the good puppet overwhelmingly. This finding indicates that babies are drawn to the nice guy and repelled by the mean guy.

In another experiment of 6 and 10 month-old infants, measuring helping versus hindering situations and using inanimate objects; a yellow square helping a blue circle up an incline and a red triangle pushing the circle down, infants prefer a helpful character to a neutral one; and prefer a neutral character to one who hinders.

Starting at about 1 year of age, babies also seem to want to lessen the pain of others. They soothe others in distress by stroking and touching or by handing over a bottle or toy. In an experiment that may suggest an inborn genetic bases for racial bias or prejudice, 3-month-olds prefer the faces of the race that is most familiar to them to those of other races. For those who are offended by the word "race" in describing human characteristics, I use the word in a cultural sense, not as a scientific meaningful term.

It seems that babies possess certain moral foundations; the capacity and willingness to judge the actions of others, some sense of justice, and the inclination to respond to altruism and selfishness.

The Artistic Human

"The artist's job is to be a witness to his time in history."
ROBERT RAUSCHENBERG

We do art; senseless acts of beauty.

The first known art work was discovered in the Blombos Cave, an archaeological site located about 300 km east of Cape Town, South Africa. The cave contains Middle Stone Age deposits currently dated at between 100,000 and 70,000 years ago.

Discoveries in this cave include thousands of pieces of ochre, an iron rich mineral material with grid or crosshatch patterns, dated to some 70,000 years ago. Some of these recovered ochre pieces have been deliberately engraved or incised and it is argued that they represent a kind of early abstract or symbolic depiction and are arguably among the most complex and clearly formed of objects claimed to be early abstract representations.

This suggested to some researchers that these early *Homo sapiens* were capable of abstraction and production of abstract art or symbolic art.

Also found there were marine gastropod shells that were deliberately pierced through the aperture, probably with a bone tool, thus enabling the making of a small sized perforation. The evidence suggests that these shells were strung, perhaps on cord or sinew and worn as a personal ornament.

Over 300 Prehistoric Cave Paintings have been discovered in Europe, India, North and South America, Africa, Australia and South East Asia.

The oldest known European cave paintings were discovered in Northern Spain in the El Castillo cave and have been dated to be more than 40,000 years old. There is debate who the artists were, *Homo sapiens* or *Homo heidelbergensis,* as well as to their purpose. As these cave showed no habitation and the paintings were located in areas deep within the cave, there is speculation that they may have some sort of communicative, religious or ceremonial significance. Other instances which we are familiar are the cave paintings of Lascaux, France which date to about 15,000 BCE.

"The aim of art is to represent not the outward appearance of things, but their inward significance"
ARISTOTLE

At some point in the history of man, the concept of ownership must have arisen. *"This is mine."* My personal and unsubstantiated view is that art grew out of the necessity of early humanoids, possibly *Homo habilis,* a million or so years ago, to claim ownership of one's tools, perhaps by making a mark on the handle of an axe or the shaft of a spear. Maybe just a X hash mark on his handle or shaft to distinguish his tool from another's; to claim ownership and authorship. Another individual might have made two hash marks, to distinguish his tool from any other. A third individual possibly made a triangle on the handle. Each could then identify one's tool. The idea of claiming ownership may have had its beginnings with a simple mark. What's left after triangle? More triangles, or squares leading to more detailed patterns. Was this the origin of art; something beyond an accidental or random pattern? Was the purpose strictly a method of coding one's own possessions? *"It's mine and I can prove it."* The act of marking an object with the intention of declaring ownership would not have occurred until the trait of self realization, selfishness and ownership arose as a human trait. Very early art may have been marks made in the dirt or sand which might have indicated directions, or perhaps marks were made upon rocks or boulders which have long disappeared due to weathering.

We cannot know if this speculation is correct nor can we say that this was the first art. We can reasonably conjecture that it may have had it's origin with the concept of self realization. When marks became representational other than only indicating ownership is what we might consider as the beginning of humans making art. It would also affirm that art ultimately triggers some kind of transcendence that can only be completed by the viewer. Art must have been the catalyst or antecedent of writing; taking a spoken word and translating symbolically into a mark on a physical object.

Not any mark could be considered art without the conscious mind knowing its purpose. An accidental mark on a stick or wall or any object is not art. Intentionality, meaning and provenance need be associated with the mark. Random marks would not be considered art, at this early stage of art development. Jackson Pollock's "Abstract Expressionism" artworks seem to be random marks but were not completely random. Yes, the paint took its own path, but thought was needed to select the color, the placement on canvas and thought given when it was complete. The uniquely continuous paint trajectories served as "fingerprints" of his motions through the air. An analysis of visual complexity of Pollock's paintings and fractals can be found in *Perceptual and Physiological Responses to Jackson Pollock's Fractals*, Taylor, et.al. Frontiers in Human Neuroscience, 2011; 5:60.

What is art? Art critic and philosopher Arthur C. Danto (1924-2013), in his book, What Art Is, examines art history with a discerning perspective. Danto discusses Duchamp's conscious effort to question aesthetic values; good or bad taste. Exemplary is Duchamp's readymades, one of which is the famous white porcelain urinal displayed as such and titled *Fountain.* Art Historians consider Duchamp's Fountain a major landmark in 20th-century art. Danto concludes "My theory is that works of art are embodied meanings. Because works like

Warhol's *Brillo Box*, I could not claim that aesthetics is part of the definition of art."

"Works of art are embodied meanings." If we accept this interpretation as to what art is; this speaks to my thought that there is a blur between early man's markings and written language; perhaps marks indicating authorship or ownership could be simply called "early written communication."

Dr. V. S. Ramachandran, Director of the Center for Brain and Cognition at the University of California, San Diego has written the book, The Tell-Tale Brain: A Neuroscientist's Quest for What Makes Us Human. In part this book provides a framework for understanding aspects of visual art, aesthetics and design. "*Our knowledge of human vision and of the brain is now sophisticated enough that we can speculate intelligently on the neural basis of art and maybe begin to construct a scientific theory of artistic experience.*"

Ramachandran, together with his collaborator, William Hirstein discuss Peak Shift, a well-known principle in animal discrimination. Peak shift is the principal that there is increased interest in a desired object when the object increases it's size. In the peak shift effect, animals sometimes respond more strongly to exaggerated versions of the training stimuli. If a rat is taught to discriminate a square from a rectangle (of say, 3:2 aspect ratio) and rewarded for the rectangle, it will soon learn to respond more frequently to the rectangle. Paradoxically, however, the rat's response to a rectangle that is even longer and skinnier (say, of aspect ratio 4:1) is even greater than it was to the original prototype on which it was trained. The rat's brain makes the leap to interpreting the appearance of greater rectangularity as being several times better. Taking this phenomenon of hyper-normal stimuli further toward art and why we respond as we do, they wonder if our brain is hardwired to appreciate art.

When you look at any evocative object, image or picture, the image is extracted by the 'early' visual areas and sent to the inferotemporal cortex; an area specialized for detecting faces and other objects. Once the object has been recognized, its emotional significance is gauged by the amygdala at the pole of the temporal lobe and if it is important, the message is relayed to the autonomic nervous system by way of the hypothalamus. Your response may be a sense of joy or flee or mate depending upon prior experiences and circumstances.

"Some artists deliberately exaggerate creative components such as shading, highlights, and illumination to an extent that would never occur in a real image to produce a caricature. These artists may be unconsciously producing heightened activity in the specific areas of the brain in a manner that is not obvious to the conscious mind."..... "Tapping into the figural primitives of our perceptual grammar and creating ultra-normal stimuli that more powerfully excite certain visual neurons in our brains as opposed to realistic-looking images." http://www.imprint.co.uk/rama/art.pdf

Producing art and appreciating art seem to be a very real human trait. It can be found in all human cultures. I have had many discussions with artists and art historians about what art is and isn't; and the answers are all very interesting, but not consistent. Art is a language; art is reflective of human's history. Art has embodied meanings.

"An artist is not paid for his labor but for his vision."
JAMES WHISTLER

From the NY Times, Nov 16, 2007 Weekend Arts: *"The Well-Shaped Phrase as Art"* by Roberta Smith - on Lawrence Weiner: *"Driven by the joy of language and quite a bit of humor, Mr. Weiner's ebullient work asks tough questions about who makes or owns art, where it can occur and how long it lasts, It reminds us that while art and money may have been inextricably entwined throughout most of history, art's real value is not measured in strings of zeros, high-priced materials or bravura skill, but in communication, experience, economy of means (the true beauty) and, yes the inspired disturbance of all status quo.*

It also affirms that art ultimately triggers some kind of transcendence that can only be completed by the viewer. Mr. Weiner has elevated Robert Rauschenberg's famous dictum to the effect that "this is art if I say so" to the more inclusive "this is art if you think so." His polymorphous efforts create situations in which such thoughts feel not only natural, they feel like our own."

I consider myself an artist; I paint and do small sculptural pieces. I'm not sure why I do this and I don't have an answer to what qualifies as art or what is a craft. I do have a desire to do art. I would consider writing this essay as a form of expression as well; maybe it's art. Not all would agree. You may find that there is no consensus what constitutes art and what falls outside the circle. I think it does not matter all that much. It does seem that many humans feel a compulsion to express themselves often by writing, painting, even doing craft work. When one is in the act of art practice, outside distractions seem to vanish. It usually requires deep concentration. For some reason, a deep feeling of accomplishment and appreciation is associated with completion.

6

Bad Traits and Behaviors

Prejudice

"Prejudice is a great time saver. You can form opinions without having to get the facts."
E.B. WHITE

"Prejudice - a vagrant opinion without visible means of support".
AMBROSE BIERCE

IN MY EARLY childhood, when I was about 7 or 8 years of age, we lived in Monterey, California. This would have been near the end of WWII. My father was a bit of a bigot. Monterey at the time had a robust sardine fishing industry and many of the fishermen were Italian and Catholic. He didn't care for Catholics or Italians. I never knew why. I remember him saying that Catholics ate fish on Fridays. I don't ever remember him eating fish on any Friday. I think he didn't want to be identified as a Catholic. I also remember that he also didn't care for Jews. He mentioned that our neighbors just down the street were Jews - stated in a manner that indicated his disdain of Jews. No reason for his dislike was given. On a day shortly after he stated this dislike, I was playing with the son of this Jewish family. I have forgotten this boy's name, but I do recall that he was about a year older and a bit larger. We must have had some sort of disagreement and he gave me a big push back. I knew that pushing him back would only escalate the situation with me ending up the loser. I immediately said, *"You're a Jew"*. He drew back *as if* I had landed the greatest of punches. Not another assault occurred. He just went home. My thought at the time was that calling him a Jew was very powerful. I caused more damage than if I had punched him back. I didn't see him or play with him after that. This incident caused me to wonder just what a Jew was. I had no idea. The word "Jew" was just a word I didn't know. I was completely ignorant. Is it not ignorance that causes man to inflict harm to others? Why do we want to inflict harm? Is it some sort of survival technique, some hard wiring in the brain? I had no intention of inflicting such pain to my friend, I just responded without thinking. Did some primitive instinct take over? Hopefully, I now know better.

Perception of Homosexuality

"Born this way..."
LADY GAGA

What great insight! Why are some humans homosexual? Why are some humans homophobic? Can we, on a whim, switch over to be homosexual? Can homosexuals be converted to heterosexuals or are they doomed? To me, as a 'straight' male, the idea of having a sexual encounter with another male is quite repulsive; to the point that I don't even want to know or think what two males do. Why is that? No one told me to think of it as repulsive. I didn't learn it. In my teens I recall hearing homophobic jokes or slanderous remarks, but I don't think this is why I am repulsed. Has genetics a role in my distaste? It seems that most males (excepting homosexuals) feel the same. Unfortunately, some individuals take this repulsion to extremes to the point of denying gays and lesbians civil rights; some to the point of becoming quite violent. Why is there this revulsion overriding our logical minds, to the point of being irrational? I might think of these bigots as ignorant, but it may have a genetic link. Those individuals *on the other team*, people who are homosexual; their behavior does have a biological origin as well.

If there were no strong urges to reproduce, the species would end. Young boys often think that kissing girls is yucky, but when puberty sets in; game change. Why is sexual coitus so enjoyable (to most)? When males see females in certain situations, we fantasize and seek opportunities to further our desire; we might have an erection. We seek out females, where ever they congregate. We head to night clubs and bars, and sure enough, there are females all dolled up looking for a husband. It seems that many males are not seeking long term commitments, but rather a one night stand. We love sex. What is it about homosexuals? Why aren't they attracted to females in the same way straight men are? Is their brain wired differently? Some people seem to think that they choose to be gay; that they are making an immoral choice, which government should discourage. Seems obvious to me; we're programmed for heterosexual relations, at least 90 percent of us are so programmed. The other 10 percent, they received an alternate program.

In 1948, Alfred Kinsey, in his book *Sexual Behavior in the Human Male* reported that 10% of the male population is gay. The actual percentage is debatable, but it is certainly not zero. Across the animal kingdom, 1,500 species including primates, exhibit homosexual behavior. Bruce Bagemihl, Biological Exuberance: Animal Homosexuality and Natural Diversity, St. Martin's Press, 1999.

Its been noted for some time that a gay man is more likely than a straight man to have a biological gay brother; lesbians are more likely than straight women to have gay sisters. http://news.stanford.edu/pr/95/950310Arc5328.html

In 1991, Simon LeVay, at The Salk Institute, first documented differences in the hypothalamus of gay and straight men. He discovered that the hypothalamus, which controls the release of sex hormones from the pituitary gland, in gay men differs from the hypothalamus in straight men. The third interstitial nucleus of the anterior hypothalamus (INAH3) was found to be more than twice as large in heterosexual men as in homosexual men.

At the Karolinska Institute, scientists studied brain scans of 90 gay and straight men and women, and considered the size of the two symmetrical halves of the brains. Heterosexual women, have symmetrical halves of similar size. Heterosexual males have slightly larger right hemispheres.

Gay males' brain resemble females in size and lesbian females have brains that resemble that of heterosexual males. The number of nerves connecting the two sides of the brains of gay men were also more like the number in heterosexual women than in straight men.

Other studies have demonstrated that a male mouse's desire to mate with either a male or a female is determined by the brain chemical serotonin, a neurotransmitter governing sexual preference in mammals. Serotonin is known to regulate sexual behaviors, such as erection, ejaculation and orgasm in both mice and men. Neuroscientist Yi Rao of Peking University and the National Institute of Biological Sciences in Beijing, and his collaborators have shown that serotonin also underlies a male's decision to woo either a female or another male. They published their results in the journal Nature. Molecular Neuroscience: *Choosing your Mate,* 1 June 2011.

Brain Development and Sexual Orientation: Colloquium Series on The Developing Brain, August 2012, University of Liége.

A large percentage of the general population feels compelled to ostracize the gay community. Biblical references are often stated. People of deep faith want to act as the moral police. With these people, ancient writings seem to outweigh the scientific literature.

There is a great deal of worldwide righteous indignation towards homosexuality and interestingly, there seems to be a particularly strong correlation between Christians and the practice of "Gay Conversion". These Christian groups seem to have the compulsion to set these gays straight. Why does a religious group seek out gays for conversion to straightness? It's a mission, a personal crusade; perhaps a path for their own redemption to the glories of heaven. There is a great deal of "sin" in the world but straightening out the gay community attracts their attention. You have probably noticed an occasional newspaper article that exposes preachers caught with pornography or with prostitutes, both male and female, and we then find that they have spent an inordinate amount of time preaching against these sins. Very strange. Do you suppose that "Gay Straighteners" (people that attempt to straighten gays) may themselves have self sex-orientation doubts? Their thinking: the best coverup of one's own personal sin is to publicly attack the sin; show them that I'm straight as an arrow. This behavior is an example of "Logic Tight Compartmentalization".

Have you ever wondered why "Gay Conversion" apparently has never worked?

A Christian group that once promoted therapy to encourage gays and lesbians to overcome their sexual preferences has closed its doors and apologized to homosexuals, acknowledging its mission had been hurtful and ignorant. Exodus International http://exodusinternational.org, the oldest and largest Christian ministry dealing with faith and homosexuality, had been operating since 1976. It announced on June 19, 2013, that it would cease operations in a statement on its website. The Irvine, California-based group's board unanimously voted to close Exodus International and begin a separate ministry, the statement said. *"I am sorry for the pain and hurt that many of you have experienced,"* President Alan Chambers said in a statement. *"I am sorry some of you spent years working through the shame and guilt when your attractions didn't change. I am sorry we promoted sexual orientation change efforts and reparative theories about sexual orientation that stigmatized parents."* Chambers said he was part of a *"system of ignorance."*

How can it be that there are homosexuals in the human (and many other species) population when they have no chance of propagating? The genes of non-propagating individuals are lost. There seems to be no positive selection for such a trait.

There are several possible explanations, one of which is that things can go wrong in a developing embryo.

In humans, the probability that each fertilized human egg survives to be born is in itself rather rare. Studies by John Opitz at the University of Utah have found that between 60 and 80 percent of all naturally conceived embryos are simply flushed out in women's normal menstrual flows unnoticed. In other studies conducted by researchers at the Stanford University School of Medicine found that 66 percent of all human embryos fail to develop successfully. Nearly all of these completely lack the biological ability to develop into anything resembling a viable baby.

One explanation is that, considering the immense number of biochemical reactions that must occur for success, things can and often do go astray. In the embryo, during the period of sexual differentiation, cells are influenced by their genetic composition and their hormonal environment. Specific genes induce gonadal differences in appropriate tissues and other genes induce structures in the brain which are important for sexual orientation, be it hetero, homo, bi, or transexual. http://www.huffingtonpost.com/2012/10/23/homosexuality--choice-born-science_n_2003361.html

Another example of events that can go "wrong" during embryonic development are the children born with indeterminate sexuality, know as intersex individuals. These people have a mixture of male and female chromosomes and genitalia. The frequency of such an event is one child per 2000. Very often surgery is performed to "correct" the outward appearance. In one case, a person with no clear gender-defining genitalia was subjected to surgery. The person said many years later: "I am neither a man nor a woman. I will remain the patchwork created by doctors, bruised and scarred." Germany has become Europe's first country to allow babies with characteristics of both sexes to be registered as neither male nor female. Parents are now allowed to leave the gender blank on birth certificates, thus creating a new category of "indeterminate sex". BBC News, Europe, 1 November 2013.

There is an abundance of scientific evidence that sexual preference and determination are genetic. Humans cannot choose how they, as embryos, develop nor can they change their genetics at some later stage in life.

Irrational Behavior

Some interesting studies have found that one of the reasons why some men act impulsively, rather than rationally, may be related to lower concentration of GABA receptors in the brain. GABA, □-Aminobutyric acid, is the primary inhibitory neurotransmitter in the mammalian central nervous system. It plays a role in regulating neuronal excitability throughout the nervous system. Men with higher levels of GABA in the prefrontal brain region have a tendency to behave calmly. Men with lower GABA levels are more likely to act aggressively, drink and take drugs in response to distress or strong emotions and urges. Interestingly, GABA is a negative regulator of dopamine function, a neurotransmitter. Dopamine plays a major role in reward-motivated behavior.

We rationalize irrational behavior. Yale researchers in a paper published in Psychological Science, Volume 18—Number 11, 2007 discuss the compulsion to justify decisions that may seem irrational. Once a decision has been made, second-guessing our decision locks that decision and prevents us from over pondering that decision. Tested humans, as well as some monkeys, seem to derogate alternatives they have chosen against, changing their current attitudes and preferences to more closely match the choices they made in previous decisions. We may all do it and it has a name; "cognitive dissonance". Providing a name, of course, doesn't help us understand the underpinning of this behavior. A perfect example is in Aesop's fable about the fox who stopped trying for the grapes, with the quip *"they were probably sour anyway."* Quipping "They're probably sour anyway", makes us feel better. Our initial choice, the grapes, being unavailable, the alternative option of walking away is just fine. So in one sense, don't personally blame a person for being irrational and unreasonable. They can't help it. They are a prime example of evolution. Don't expect them to change, to see the light, to be logical and to reason out the problem.

Stubborn

"I'm not stubborn. My way is just better."
MAYA BANKS

We all seem to know when someone is stubborn or is a risk taker. We usually associate stubborn behavior as a detrimental behavior; displayed when someone who forges ahead without sufficient caution or knowledge of the consequences. Risk takers we associate with individuals such as David Farragut, a Flag Officer during the American Civil War that gave the order: *"Damn the torpedoes, full steam ahead"*, on August 5, 1864, during his siege of Mobile Bay. After one of his ships sank in the heavily mined bay and the rest of his fleet pulling back, Farragut gave the order: "*Damn the torpedoes. Four bells. Captain Drayton, go ahead! Full speed!"* The bulk of the fleet entered the bay and were triumphant. Tethered naval mines at the time were known as torpedoes.

Stubbornness must be an inherited trait of humans. Sometimes it's forging ahead without fully considering the consequences, all for a future good; foreseeing a future we want. Obviously, knowledge of consequences and a bit of luck favors a positive outcome. Entrepreneurs, who risk their time on unproven ideas may have a bit of a stubborn streak. Calculated risk may result in a positive outcome, unrealizable without taking the chance.

Other times stubbornness is exhibited when an individual is unwilling to consider alternate explanations which are contrary to one's strongly held belief, usually religious or political. Regardless of how persuasive one's arguments may be, a stubborn individual will close off conversation. You will be talking to a brick wall. It would be difficult to design an experiment to identify the neurological pathways for risk taking and stubbornness but they may have similar loci in the brain.

Denial and Deniers

> *"It's not denial. I'm just selective about the reality I accept".*
> - Bill Watterson, creator of *Calvin and Hobbes*

The question that comes to me is: Do Sean Hannity and Rush Limbaugh, conservative media personalities, truly believe that the Climate Crisis is a hoax? Alternatively, are they "playing" with their conservative base in the manner of shysters that sell snake oil to naive and gullible people knowing full well that it is useless? Huge audiences equates to big money. Are they deniers with economic objectives, because to behave otherwise would evaporate their base or are they deniers in a clinical sense; deniers in the same fashion as Holocaust deniers and some alcoholics? We may never know.

Denial is a self preservation mechanism, a coping mechanism which allows one time to adjust to or minimize a painful or stressful issue. Denial is an unconscious process where the brain prohibits perception. There is an interesting book; Denial: Self-Deception, False Beliefs, and the Origins of the Human

Mind, by Ajit Varki and Danny Brower. They argue that denial is a prerequisite for human intellectual development. Empathy is the awareness of another, which can only occur when, evolutionarily, we are aware of ourselves. The ability to deny reality, including denying death, our mortality or the denial of events was a factor for self-realization. "Denial of reality is an essential skill for us to function normally in the world. It is a fundamental property of being human."

Anger and Aggression

"Anger dwells only in the bosom of fools"
ALBERT EINSTEIN

"Whatever is begun in anger ends in shame"
BENJAMIN FRANKLIN

There are many areas of research under the general heading of neuroscience. One such area of interest currently is the research examining the role of genetics and the environment as it affects behavior in humans and animals. For centuries, it has been observed that just as it is in many animals, birds, dogs, fish and mice, aggressive behavior can be selected and bred.

Self-righteousness or sanctimoniousness is a feeling of some individuals when of confronted with beliefs that are contradictory on to one's own beliefs. Self-righteous behavior is likely when one judges their beliefs superior or have greater virtue than another's beliefs. Onset of these felling may result from mis-understanding, mis- communication or selective or false memories. It may result from an egocentric defensive reflex. Self-righteous attitudes are often the root cause of anger and aggression.

With contemporary scientific techniques, DNA can be isolated, cloned and sequenced as can the protein coded by most any gene; both can then be carefully analyzed. Many neurotransmitters, chemicals that transmit signals from a neuron to the appropriate cell, and their receptors have been cloned and sequenced and subsequently investigated. These neurotransmitters and receptors control human behavior.

Serotonin is a neurotransmitter and thought to play a role in the feeling of both happiness and aggression. Selected male mice, carrying a mutant variant for the serotonin gene, exhibit greater than normal aggression when, for example another male mouse is placed in its cage. However, these mice exhibit normal behavior when their environment is non-stressful.

Another neurotransmitter, one of over 3 dozen identified, is dopamine, a very common biochemical chemical found in invertebrates on up to humans. Dopamine plays a role in behavior, cognition and in reward-motivated behavior. Rewards such as food and sex as well as addictive drugs amplify the effects of dopamine. Schizophrenia involves altered levels of dopamine activity and antipsychotic drugs have their primary effect by attenuating dopamine activity.

A protein, named DARPP-32 and found in the brain, is associated with antisocial and addictive behaviors. A research team, led by Martin Reuter, Department of Psychology, University of Bonn, Bonn, Germany, published an article in the journal: Behavioral Brain Research, 202 (2) entitled: "*The Biological Basis of Anger...*" DARPP-32 regulates the dopamine signaling pathway. When the brain's dopamine level is elevated, test animals are quicker to display anger and aggression. In humans there are two naturally occurring DNA variants to the DARPP-32 gene, the difference being very small, just two base pairs. Human subjects were tested using a questionnaire to assay how disposed they were to respond to a stressful situation with anger. There was a correlation with DNA sequence and anger assessment. One group with one sequence had a higher level of anger assessment, while the other group with the other DNA sequence scored lower. A variation in just one tiny section of the gene may have a direct affect human behavior and DARPP-32 may be the key to understanding why some people display greater anger than others.

Another gene that is linked to aggression codes for the enzyme monoamine oxidase A. This enzyme regulates the amount of serotonin in the brain. Some individuals that have a variation of this gene, produce less of the monoamine oxide A enzyme and tend to be significantly more impulsive and aggressive. The expression of the gene is environmentally dependent; it is triggered by stressful experiences; an example that genes may be expressed differently depending on the environment. You may have a strong urge to do harm, but the teachings of your mother or the presence of a police officer may alter your behavior.

While we may conclude that aggressiveness is a genetic trait, we cannot determine if any one individual will have violent impulses or behave passively. An important ethical and social question is to what extent should criminal sentencing consider the genetic predisposition of an individual. Should genetic testing be considered in sentencing or possibly in rehabilitation programs? Should adults or children with a biological marker for violence be identified?

I would think that *Homo sapiens* survived in part, because we have the genetic information to be aggressive. In our ancestral past, there likely were overlaps temporally and geographically with other similar but distinct humanoid species. Undoubtedly there would have been competition for resources.

Fear and Loathing in the Amygdala

There was a cartoon in the July 29, 2013, The New Yorker, magazine that seemed appropriate for the subject of fear. The cartoon depicts the cover of a fictional magazine, one which you might find on the newsstand alongside the tabloids displayed at the supermarket checkout. The fictional magazine is titled *"New Dread, the Magazine of Undiscovered Fears"*. Featured on the cover are the titles of articles within the magazine: *The Ten Reasons to Avoid Bananas, Should Sofas Be Banned? The Case against Flannel* and, *Is Your Tea putting you at Risk?*

Knowing some humans, this magazine might sell quite well. Why are we, some of us, at times overcome with fear? Where in the brain is fear central?

The emotion that we know as fear arose millions of years ago in more primitive animals. In evolutionarily older brains, the reptile brain for example, sensory information travels directly and quickly from the thalamus to the amygdala where it elicits the autonomic and motor responses we call fear. The old fast system persists because a behavioral response at the first hint of danger is of little consequence when mistaken, but may mean the difference between life and death when appropriate. Ledoux, J. (1996). Emotion Theory and Research, *Annual Review of Psychology*, Vol. 60.

"It is hard, I submit, to loathe bloodshed, including war, more than I do, but it is still harder to exceed my loathing of the very nature of totalitarian states in which massacre is only an administrative detail."

VLADIMIR NABOKOV

Loathing is something else. It's a step beyond hate, it's disgust raised to a high level. Loathing is way beyond aversion or repugnance.

Hunter S. Thompson, in his 1972 book: Fear and Loathing in Las Vegas: A savage Journey to the Heart of the American Dream, used the combination of fear and loathing in two manners. In the context of the story, the term refers to the abundant consumption of drugs; hallucinogens, alcohol, and narcotics. It was also an underlining commentary of the decadence of American society into moral degeneracy and hypocritical hedonism, largely due to the misguided and greed-driven leadership of national politicians, officers of the law, and local authorities.

Rage, Revenge and Vindictiveness

This is certain, that a man that studieth revenge keeps his wounds green, which otherwise would heal and do well."
FRANCIS BACON

Family feuds, dysfunctional families, brother versus brother, fights that last decades, sometimes the duration of their lives; even generational intra-family battles; what's going on? Individuals displaying this sort of behavior are accusatory, exhibit warped memories regarding relevant events and react in a vindictive manner. They won't consider alternative explanations and logic and reason are beyond their grasp. Rage increases as a function of time. Most people know of such occurrences; there're not that rare. When encountering such a situation, it may be better to just walk away. Speculation is that these individuals may have genotypes a bit different from the norm that predispose them to such behavior. Change may not be possible.

There are many factors to consider regarding rage episodes: how we previously responded to a similar experience; what we have been taught or have learned from past experience; our ability to rationally think of all possible alternative explanations for the slight we received; our understanding of the possible consequences of any action we may take or not take. These are all factors that determine our actions to any episode that could result in rage, revenge or vindictive behavior. Other explanations might include miscommunication or confusion of words or signals or faulty or selective memories, or insufficient information. Alternatively, unreasonable behavior, such as rage or revenge may be caused by biochemical or anatomical "imbalance" in their brain.

There might be anatomical or biochemical differences within our species that account for the differences in human responses to environmental stresses. There are a plethora of personality disorders that are recognized in The Diagnostic and Statistical Manual of Mental Disorders manual published by the *American Psychiatric Association.* The manual describes these disorders that cause people to have limited capabilities in their ability to function normally.

An example is *Oppositional Defiant Disorder*, a childhood disorder in which there is an ongoing pattern of anger-guided disobedience, hostility, and defiant behavior toward authority figures which goes beyond the bounds of normal childhood behavior. Children suffering from this disorder may appear very stubborn and often angry and it has been associated with aggressive, impulsive, and antisocial personality.

Delusion

Humans are susceptible to delusions that range from the mild, *"I'm sure my horse will win the race"* to the severe. The clinically recognized *Delusion Disorder* is such as where the patient suffers from persistent delusions that could not possibly be true and the symptoms persist for at least one month. The non-bizarre delusions typically are beliefs of something occurring in a person's life which is not out of the realm of possibility, yet have no veracity. For example, conspiracy theories, spousal cheating, someone will harm you or is spying on you. Fact checking can dispel these beliefs for the rational. The human brain has evolved to have a heightened sense of fear; a threat detection system. The intensity to which we respond is dependent upon the degree of sensitivity we have to a threat and whether we fact check or look for additional evidence. If that system becomes oversensitive, the result is paranoia. The physical and chemical makeup and of course our environmental experiences may determine how we respond. Political operatives may just be using our susceptibility to delusion to advance their cause. Just a thought.

"New Rule: Conspiracy theorists who are claiming that we didn't really kill Bin Laden must be reminded that they didn't think he did the crime in the first place."
BILL MAHER

Why do some rational people accept as true not only one Conspiracy Theory but their whole world-view seems dominated by numerous conspiracies? One research poll conducted by Fairleigh Dickinson University found that 62 percent of registered American voters believe in at least one political conspiracy theory. Dr. Viren Swami, psychology professor at the University of Westminster, England suggests that believing that one theory is plausible you might feel that other theories are plausible even if they contradict one another. It seems contagious. Some individuals seem to turn on a "belief system" that convinces them that evil forces are prevalent. *"The best predictor of belief in conspiracy theory is belief in other conspiracy theories."* It's not so much a response to a single event as it is an expression of an overarching worldview. Not an explanation, but his observation is that even sane people have the capacity to develop incredible narratives. He finds that conspiracy theorists seem to be individuals with low self esteem; they believe the world as a whole is filled with deviants. It is the strategy by which these individuals deal with uncertainty and the feeling of being powerless. There are two interesting phenomena, one called *confirmation bias* where there is a tendency to pay greater attention to evidence that supports what you already believe. The other, an alternative condition, is called the *backfire effect* when efforts to invalidate information especially of a political nature, often backfires, leaving people even more convinced that their initial position has veracity.

Behavioral traits arose early on in our evolution and evolved into what we experience today. Good and bad behaviors have their roots in our genetic heritage; they are in a sense, predictable by our DNA. What is clear is that the way people behave results from a complex interaction between a great number of genetic, social and environmental factors. Genes determine the general structure and chemicals of the brain, and genes determine how the brain reacts to experience. Experience is required to enrich the matrix of synaptic connections, especially during critical periods of brain development. Individuals raised in an environment of higher levels of stimulation, especially during critical periods of development, have increased numbers of synapses with greater complexity. Youngsters raised in a sensory deprived environment, such as we have read about in some old Soviet style orphanages, have delayed and impaired cognitive development. Individuals with higher education who participate in cognitively stimulation activities have a greater resilience to the effects of aging and dementia.

Recently, the nature versus nurture debate has entered the realm of law and criminal defense. In some cases, lawyers for violent offenders have begun to argue that an individual's genes, rather than their rational decision-making processes, can cause criminal activity. The most dominant position by many is that although genes may increase the propensity for criminality, they do not determine it

7

Man's Inhumanity to Man

'Many and sharp the num'rous ills
Inwoven with our frame!
More pointed still we make ourselves
Regret, remorse, and shame!
And Man, whose heav'n-erected face
The smiles of love adorn, -
Man's inhumanity to man
Makes countless thousands mourn!"

ROBERT BURNS - MAN WAS MADE TO MOURN: A DIRGE, (1785)

UNFORTUNATELY, THROUGHOUT HISTORY, and even today, there have been a few *Homo sapiens* practitioners of horrendous and immoral acts. We are the only species capable of attaining high levels of atrocities. We have the intellectual capacity to invent and implement schemes that create pain and suffering. We have the mental skills to recognize grotesque pain in others. Thankfully, we are the only species that has this capacity. What follows are just a few of the behaviors that illustrate man's inhumanity to man. This review is to reinforce the contention that we are not all that nobel a species.

Slavery

Ingenious was the fellow who discovered how to make rope. I would conjecture that the invention of rope was a feat that changed the outcome of human history. The first sort of rope was probably made of woven vegetation; vines or long palm leaves or sliced slivers of animal skin into a binding material. Rope had many uses. Rope could lash sticks together as part of the structure of a shelter, be the handle of baskets to ease hauling goods. By lashing together the front legs and the rear legs of a killed animal, then slung on a pole, tribe members could share the load back to their home.

Rope could have enabled these people to bind into subservience captured members of a hostile tribe or another hominid competing species. This discovery would have enabled the tribe to take hostages and force them to do the menial work. Slavery, most likely arose early in the path on to modern humans. Rope was one of the inventions that changed the world.

Modern slavery may be a much larger problem than recently estimated. More Than 29 million people around the world live as slaves, as stated in the Global Slavery Index. The index considers both children and adults to be "living in slavery" if they have been victims of sex or debt bondage, mandated marriages or forced labor.

http://www.globalslaveryindex.org

Torture

'The wish to hurt, the momentary intoxication with pain, is the loophole through which the pervert climbs into the minds of ordinary men."

Jacob Bronowski

The complete history of man would need to include the history of torture. Torture is, what most intelligent humans would conclude, a very dark chapter of humankind; a chapter that must have predated recorded history and continues to the present.

The purposes of torture seem to have several agenda: to extract confessions from prisoners, to punish, or cause fear to anyone contemplating doing a forbidden act or the sadistic act that bring some sort of pleasure to the torturer or his leader.

Methods of torture have continually improved, so to speak. Methods have included those of which you may be familiar, but only by your reading, hopefully. Included here is a small selection of the "ingenious" methods man has concocted to torment others. Examining one's history may give a perspective that could alter future events; not to make the same mistake.

Stating that humans are not animals, may just well be a tribute to *"the animals"*.

The rack, was used to extract the names of the conspirators to assassinate Emperor Nero from the freedwoman, Epicharis in 65 C.E. The rack was used during the Inquisition, starting in the 12th century in France to combat the spread of religious sectarianism.

On the rack, the victim's limbs are strapped to a device that allows the torturer, by means of pulleys to very gradually, in steps, to increase the tension on the limbs inducing excruciating pain. Eventually, the victim's bones are dislocated with a loud crack, caused by snapping cartilage, ligaments or bones. If the torturer kept turning the handles the limbs would eventually be torn off.

The Iron Maiden was first used in the Ming Dynasty (1368–1644). The disloyal prisoner would be locked into an iron containment which was suspended over hot coals. The executioner would pour water onto hot coals. The steam was a certain and painful death.

Dunking was widely used during The Tribunal of the Holy Office on the Inquisition, commonly known as the Spanish Inquisition. The Tribunal was established in 1482 by King Ferdinand and Queen Isabella, famous for financing the 1492 voyages of Christopher Columbus. Dunking was used to insure adherence to the Christian faith of Muslims and Jews. During the Salem Witch trials, between February 1692 and May 1693, dunking was a punishment for sorcery, and usually "favored" women.

King Henry VIII shared in the history of torture. In 1532 he made boiling a legal form of capital punishment.

Other creative methods of doing away with the unwanted ones was freezing, by forcing a victim to stand outside, in winter, naked with cold water poured their head. Live burial had the victim buried up to his neck followed by stoning, or pouring honey on them and allowing ants or other animals to feast.

Water Boarding is a form of torture in which water is poured over cloth covering the face and breathing passages of an immobilized captive, causing the individual to experience the sensation of suffocation and drowning.

In the *Age of Enlightenment*, a period of western intellectual history (the late 17th to the late 18th centuries), the practice of water boarding was banned. The populace found it "morally repugnant,"

Unfortunately it just didn't disappear. Darius Rejali, a professor at Reed College in Oregon and author of the book, Torture and Democracy says, water boarding has been an interrogation technique preferred by the world's democracies, including past White House officials. It is an attractive interrogation technique, as it causes great physical and mental suffering, yet leaves no marks on the body.

In recent years, it wasn't merely low-level brutalizers and their immediate superiors who sanctioned and approved torture techniques, but senior White House officials, including National Security Adviser Condoleezza Rice and Vice President Dick Cheney. To spruce up the term to sound very appealing, they changed the term to *Enhanced Interrogation.* In addition to water boarding, these compassionate conservatives also used hypothermia, stress positions, electroshock and intimidation by barking snarling dogs.

The argument against water boarding often cites Abu Zubaydah who was water boarded 83 times while being interrogated by the United States CIA. He began releasing information after only 35 seconds. However, it was later found that he was lying and making up information to stop the torture; an example of its uselessness as a method of obtaining reliable information. Condoleezza Rice told the CIA, that these harsher interrogation tactics were acceptable. In September 2009, the Obama administration acknowledged, during Abu Zubaydah's habeas corpus petition, that Abu Zubaydah had never been a member of al-Qaeda, nor involved in the attacks on the African embassies in 1998, nor the attacks on the United States on September 11, 2001. He has never been charged in the US. He remains a captive at Guantanamo.

Internment and Concentration Camps. The U.S. government set up internment camps for the Cherokee and other Native Americans in the 1830s. During World War II, Nazi Germany expanded the term to include extermination camps; places where millions of ordinary people were enslaved as part of their war effort, often starved, tortured and killed. In the United States, 110,000 Japanese/Americans were "interned" in camps across the USA. The reason, their crime; appearing physically similar to the Japanese that attached Pearl Harbor. The conservative mindset at the time was that of fear, without the use of logic, reason or compassion.

Apartheid was a system of racial segregation in South Africa from 1948 to 1994. Nelson Mandela (1918-2013), is credited as being the inspirational leader which led to the ending of apartheid. In 1962 he was arrested, convicted of conspiracy to overthrow the government, and sentenced to life imprisonment. He served 27 years in prison. In 1986, in reaction to apartheid, the United States Congress passed and sent to President Ronald Reagan the Comprehensive Anti-Apartheid Act, which banned bank loans, and the trade of numerous goods. Ronald Reagan vetoed the bill, but was overridden by the Republican controlled Senate.

Ethnic Cleansing,

"This is what men do when they aspire to the knowledge of gods,"

Jacob Bronowski as he stood in front of the remains of the crematoriums at Auschwitz and dips his hands in the pond containing the ashes of some of the people murdered there, who included members of his own family.

The motivations for ethnic cleansing have been stated as: "they" have a different god and it is our *God's Will* that we do away with them; or "they" control all the banking and we are left with next to nothing or they took our lands and we'll do anything to get the land back, or a combination of such excuses.

Some perpetrators of torture may be mere underlings carrying out the orders of higher ups. They may have no choice but to obey or face similar consequences; people that, in their ordinary home environment, are quite peace loving individuals. Is this human characteristic the result of our genetic heritage? Did their mothers teach their children the fine art of torture?

"The play of tolerance opposes the principle of monstrous certainty that is endemic to fascism and, sadly, not just fascism but all the various faces of fundamentalism. When we think we have certainty, when we aspire to the knowledge of the gods, then Auschwitz can happen and can repeat itself. Arguably, it has repeated itself in the genocidal certainties of past decades."
SIMON CRITCHLEY, AN ENGLISH PHILOSOPHER

Condoning and conducting torture; there is a plethora of Dick Cheney-like humans. Should we assign the cause of this behavior to high testosterone levels, psychopathic disorders, sadistic or orgasmic seekers or maybe these humans just lack empathy?

A total list of methods and descriptions of torture is far greater than where I would like to take you. *Homo sapiens* are capable of the most heinous methods to dominate other humans. Why did I relate all this to you? To reinforce the notion that humans can do the horrible. A benchmark to which we should never sink, ever.

War

"War does not determine who is right - only who is left."
BERTRAND RUSSELL

"It is forbidden to kill; therefore all murderers are punished unless they kill in large numbers and to the sound of trumpets."
VOLTAIRE

We have seen bumper stickers that state "Pray for World Peace"; a world where there are no wars. This seems to be everyone's wish. What if humans never ever waged war; no one was sent off to war, no one killed in war?

Considering only a few of the USA's wars: The Civil War, 620,000 soldiers died. World War I, 16,000,000, died. War War II, 60,000,000 people died. Just these three wars, more than 76,000,000 individuals died. Not included are the Korean war, Vietnam, Gulf "wars" or other "police actions" or all the blood shed over at least 10,000 plus years; 1000's of wars. The number of young men and women killed in all the world wars must be in the high hundreds of millions, maybe billions; men and women that did not breed. Their contribution to the world population had they not died, but lived and bred would, I guess, have added billions more people. The world population would be at least 10 times greater that today's population of 7 Billion inhabitants. War: a blessing for population control advocates.

So in a demonic sense, war is good for the human species; it keeps, or at least slows, humans from over populating the earth. Along with population control, war increases employment. The Military Industrial complex, remember? Without hundreds of overseas military bases, without Halliburton and similar corporations along with the Armed Services, unemployment would soar. The wars of *Homo sapiens* have been a culling success. I guess the take home lesson is: War is good. So what will your response be when next you see that bumper sticker, "Keep Peace Alive"?

In the Sunday, February 13, 2011 installment of Gary Trudeau's comic strip *Doonesbury*, Mark Slackmeyer, a longtime character in the strip who is a liberal radio host makes a point about gun violence.

"What are we like as a people?" Slackmeyer muses to himself in his studio. *"Nine years ago we were attacked -- 3,000 people died. In response, we started two long, bloody wars and built a vast homeland-security apparatus -- all at a cost of trillions! Now consider this. During those same nine years, 270,000 Americans were killed by gunfire at home. Our response? We weakened our gun laws."*

Prisons

"It is said that no one truly knows a nation until one has been inside its jails. A nation should not be judged by how it treats its highest citizens, but its lowest ones."

Nelson Mandela

There certainly is a need to incarcerate certain individuals. Many of the incarcerated began life as moral individuals, but due to circumstances, poor upbringing, lack of education and the unavailability of decent jobs, they end up in the prison system. Worldwide there are a great variety of prisons, from the more lenient, with goals of rehabilitation to the severe, used as a facility to inflict punishment.

The United States is number one in the world, in pro rata incarceration. There are 2.24 million people in prison in the U.S. More than one of every one hundred Americans is in prison; the majority for drug offenses, mainly marijuana. One in every three black males born today can expect to go to prison at some point in their life, compared with one in every six Latino males, and one in every 17 white males. Racial minorities are more likely than white Americans to be arrested. Once arrested, they are more likely to be convicted; and once convicted, they are more likely to face stiff sentences. There are 3,281 prisoners in America serving life sentences for nonviolent crimes with no chance of parole. For Profit Corporations such as Corrections Corp of America and GEO Group are the leaders in the correction's industry. It's a 70 billion dollar industry. These corporations spend millions of dollars lobbying States and Congress to stiffen sentencing. Privatization of our prison system has the intended purpose of lowering costs. The "unintended" consequence of all penal systems is suppressing the black and Latino vote. A form of political shenanigans, "modern" slavery or bigotry perhaps? http://www.sentencingproject.org

Contrary to the United States, Sweden will be closing four prisons as there has been a drop in their prison population. Two factors have been attributed to the decline. One is Sweden's liberal prison approach, with its strong focus on rehabilitating prisoners. The other factor is that Swedish courts have given more lenient sentences for drug offenses. Erwin James, The Guardian, November 11, 2013. Is there a lesson to be learned?

8

Man's Inhumanity to the Planet

'Many and sharp the numerous ills
Inwoven with our frame!
More pointed still we make ourselves
Regret, remorse, and shame!
And Man, whose heav'n-erected face
The smiles of love adorn, -
Man's inhumanity to man
Makes countless thousands mourn!

ROBERT BURNS, FROM MAN WAS MADE TO MOURN: A DIRGE, 1785:

Climate Crisis

"One of the difficulties in examining the issue of the climate change and greenhouse gases is that there is a wide range of scientific opinion on this issue and the science community does not agree to the extent of the problem or the critical threshold of when this problem is truly catastrophic."

REP. DARRELL ISSA (R-CA-49), CHAIRMAN OF THE HOUSE JUDICIARY COMMITTEE AND THE OVERSIGHT AND GOVERNMENT REFORM COMMITTEE: PROJECT VOTE SMART ISSUE POSITION, JANUARY 1, 2012.

NOT ONLY HAVE humans inflicted pain and suffering on other humans, we have been poor custodians of this planet. Alarming is the apparent disconnect between reality and human's perception of reality. Powerful individuals and corporations are spending billions of dollars for their own self interest, ignoring the threat of the climate crisis. This will be an examination of the crises and the root causes. There is urgency, as if we do nothing, the consequences just might be enormous for all humans.

Why is carbon dioxide called a greenhouse gas? Avid gardeners would certainly know about greenhouses, especially those living in more northern (and southern) latitudes. A greenhouse, sometimes referred to as a glasshouse, is a garden structure paneled with glass as the roof and glass on the other 4 sides. Visible light shines through the glass of the greenhouse, and is absorbed as infrared energy by the soil and the plants. The heat, in the form of infrared radiation, is partially trapped inside the greenhouse, as the glass is not completely transparent to these wave lengths; it is partially opaque to this spectrum of radiation.

Carbon dioxide and methane gases in our atmosphere are similar to the glass in the greenhouse. These gases that are in the atmosphere, reflect back to earth some of the radiation that strikes the earth during daylight hours that otherwise would have radiated back out into space in dark of the night. The greater the concentration of greenhouse gas in the atmosphere, the greater the amount of heat trapped, BTU's if you prefer. Simplistically, all the energy in the form of visible light that reaches the earth is radiated back out into space at night, except for the trapped heat energy. Without this re-radiation back into space the earth would continue to heat up.

The most consequential greenhouse gases in our atmosphere are carbon dioxide and methane. Nitrogen and oxygen together comprise 99 percent of our atmosphere; however they are transparent to infrared radiation, hence are not greenhouse gases. Methane is of considerable concern as it is 20 times more opaque to infrared radiation than carbon dioxide. Methane in our atmosphere predominately has a biogenic origin, a byproduct of the decay of vegetation. Cows, humans and other animals also expel methane gas as a consequence of their diet. The International Panel on Climate Change's Fifth Assessment

Report projects that there will be a drastic increase of methane levels as the arctic regions warm, the frozen tundra thaws and the ancient plants, tundra, decay releasing methane as a byproduct.

Carbon dioxide in the atmosphere, to a large extend is the result of humans activity. The carbon cycle is the balance of carbon dioxide in the atmosphere, the oceans and the biosphere, a flux of production and uptake. Natural production of this gas results from volcanic activity, the combustion of organic matter including wildfires and the respiration of living aerobic organisms. The leading cause of anthropogenic sources of carbon dioxide is from the burning of fossil fuels. Other sources are the industrial production of cement and deforestation.

Our oceans and inland waters are a natural sink for carbon dioxide, resulting in their acidification, essentially our waters are becoming more carbonated and hence more acidic. This acidification of our oceans is a significant problem for marine calcifying organisms, such as coral and some plankton as they become vulnerable to dissolution as the oceans become more acidic. As the coral reefs disappear, so will most smaller fish. The whole oceanic food chain is threatened. Ocean acidification is associated with some of the worst crises in biotic history. The Permian extinction took place roughly two hundred and fifty million years ago and killed off nearly ninety percent of all organisms on the planet. This drastic kill-off was cause by increased volcanism which resulted in drastic increases on carbon dioxide and methane gases, ocean acidification, sea level changes and shifting in ocean circulation driven by climate change. The carbon dioxide levels reached 2,000 ppm, five times present levels.

In 1750, at the beginning of the Industrial Revolution, the concentration of carbon dioxide in the atmosphere was 280 parts per million. In 1960 the level was 320 ppm; the 2006 level equaled 381 ppm. An instrument near the summit of Mauna Loa in Hawaii has recorded a long-awaited climate milestone: the amount of carbon dioxide in the atmosphere there has exceeded 400 parts per million (ppm) for the first time in 55 years of measurement—and probably more than the last 3 million years of Earth history. That's a 43 percent increase since 1750. The latest new climate-change report from the United Nations states that sea levels could rise by more than 3 feet and could reach 6 feet by the end of the 21st century and that there is a 95% likelihood that the global warming that is causing this rise is largely a result of human activity.

"I have offered compelling evidence that catastrophic global warming is a hoax. That conclusion is supported by the painstaking work of the nation's top climate scientists."
SEN. JIM INHOFE (R-OK) RANKING MEMBER OF THE U.S. SENATE ENVIRONMENT AND PUBLIC WORKS COMMITTEE. JULY 9, 2003.

Out of 11,944 peer-reviewed scientific studies on climate change, 97.2% agree that it's real and humans are causing it. John Cook et al. 2013 *Environ. Res. Lett. 8 024024.*

If Eleven Thousand Nine Hundred and Forty-four home fire studies stated that the probability of your home would burn down to the ground within the next few years was 97.2%, would you not buy home fire insurance? You could save a few dollars by declining to purchase fire insurance, with the assertion that they may be wrong; that these experts are perpetuating a hoax, or we need greater consensus.

Humans are adding more than 35 billion metric tons of carbon dioxide to the atmosphere each year. *AtmosNews,* University Corporation for AtmosphericResearch, May 15, 2013. That is equivalent to 100 million tons of carbon dioxide per day. Converting tons to pounds: 200,000,000,000 pounds carbon dioxide per day, every day. Yikes!

Our atmosphere is huge, but adding 100 million tons today and another 100 million tons tomorrow; can one doubt that there would not be terrible consequences? There is a direct positive correlation between atmosphere carbon dioxide concentration and global temperatures calibrated over the last four hundred thousand years.

"The observational data show that the frequency of unusually warm anomalies has been increasing decade by decade over the past three decades. The location of these extreme warm anomalies is dependent upon variable meteorological patterns, but the decade-by-decade movement of the bell curve to the right, and the emergence of an increased number of extreme warm anomalies, is an expression of increasing global warming. The continuing planetary

energy imbalance and the rapid increase of CO2 emissions from fossil fuel use assure that global warming will continue on decadal time scales."
HTTP://WWW.NASA.GOV/PDF/719139MAIN_2012_GISTEMP_SUMMARY.PDF

The International Energy Agency predicts that, without efforts to stabilize atmospheric concentrations of greenhouse gas, average global temperature rise is projected to be at least 6°C in the long term. The U.S. Navy predicts that summers in the Arctic may be ice-free by 2016. http://www.theguardian.com/environment/earth-insight/2013/dec/09/us-navy-arctic-sea-ice-2016-melt

"Two thousand years of published human histories say that warm periods were good for people. It was the harsh, unstable Dark Ages and Little Ice Age that brought bigger storms, untimely frost, widespread famine and plagues of disease."
SENIOR FELLOW DENNIS AVERY, HUDSON INSTITUTE, AN AMERICAN CONSERVATIVE NONPROFIT THINK TANK BASED IN WASHINGTON, D.C.

The consequences of increased global temperatures will be numerous and ominous. The temperate forests will dry (further) which facilitates insects growth, which kills the trees which increases the probability and severity of forest fires. The frequency of grasslands burning will increase. The oceans are warming more rapidly than any time during the past 10,000 years. We are carbonating the oceans. As the earth warms, expect decreases in potable water supplies and agricultural production, especially in some of the least developed countries. In Africa within the next decade, between 75 and 250 million humans will suffer increased water stress. Agricultural production could be reduced by up to 50 percent in Africa. In Europe coastal flooding will occur, resulting in lower food production. In Latin America, there will be a replacement of forest by savannah; resulting in a loss of biodiversity. Agriculture will suffer. The U.N.'s Nobel-winning Intergovernmental Panel On Climate Change (IPCC) http://www.ipcc.ch, predicts climate change will cut food production by 2% world-wide each decade through the rest of the century. Meanwhile, global food demand is projected to rise 14% over the same period. The death rate from disease associated with floods and droughts are expected to rise in some regions. Worldwide, expect flood damage to the infrastructure as storms increase in severity.

As the Arctic ice melts it leaves less reflective oceanic waters exposed, which, of course, absorb additional heat. Warming of the oceans increases the occurrence of hurricanes. What should be very worrisome to northern Americans, Canadians and Europeans is the fresh water resulting from the arctic melt. The polar ice cap and Greenland hold enormous amounts of fresh water. The Gulf Stream, warm saltwater moving north from the tip of Florida, follows the eastern coastline of the United States and Newfoundland before crossing the Atlantic Ocean to the west coast of northern Europe. This warm water increases summer and winter temperature along our eastern seaboard and northern European countries. The resultant fresh water from the arctic melt moving into the salty warm northern end of the Gulf Stream will be a barricade to the Stream's normal flow. Blockage will leave Europe with colder winters and summers. Food production will suffer as a consequence. Undoubtedly there will be food shortages. Presently there is a sever drought in California and the West. Decisions must be made: water for farmers and ranchers or water for citizens.

Did I leave out any other cataclysmic effects of our climate crisis?

Of course I did. Billions of people now live in or near coastal regions of the world. They certainly will need to move to higher ground.

There are over a half billion people that live in low lying littoral areas surrounding the Bay of Bengal; eastern India, Bangladesh, Sri Lanka, Myanmar, Thailand, Malaysia and Sumatra. http://www.nytimes.com/2013/10/14/opinion/the-bay-of-bengal-in-peril-from-climate-change.html

Bangladesh, one of these low lying countries with a population of 160 million is in grave danger of flooding from rising sea levels. When the flooding occurs and great areas are below sea level, I feel confident that India will extend a warm invitation, welcoming the people of Bangladesh to come on over with a hearty: *"Welcome! We have plenty"*. Oops, sorry, the whole eastern section of India will be under oceanic water as well. No doubt that there will be food shortages. Will food fights lead to a nuclear holocaust, or to *just* conventional warfare?

A recent slowdown in global warming has led some skeptics to renew their claims that industrial carbon emissions are not causing a century-long rise in

Earth's surface temperatures. Counterpoint: *"With global warming you don't see a gradual warming from one year to the next,"* said Kevin Trenberth, a climate scientist at the National Center for Atmospheric Research in Boulder, Colorado. *"It's more like a staircase. You trot along with nothing much happening for 10 years and then suddenly you have a jump and things never go back to the previous level again."* The study adds support to the idea that the oceans are taking up some of the excess heat, at least for the moment. Science, 1 November 2013.

"Perhaps you notice how the denial is so often the preface to the justification."
CHRISTOPHER HITCHENS

Who is denying the climate crisis? 158 elected representatives in the 113th Congress, all Republicans, have publicly declared that climate change is not caused by man. These same Republicans have taken over $51 million from the fossil fuel industry that's driving the carbon emissions which cause climate change.

ExxonMobil and other fossil fuel corporations have combined with traditionally conservative corporate groups like the U.S. Chamber of Commerce and conservative foundations like the Koch brothers' Americans for Prosperity, to raise doubts about the basic validity of what is, essentially, a settled scientific truth. That message gets amplified by conservative think tanks — like the Cato Institute and the American Enterprise Institute — and then picked up by conservative media outlets such as *Fox News* as well as conservative websites. Time Magazine, *October 04, 2011.*

The Koch brothers revealed that they have contributed $67 million dollars to climate-denial front groups. National Geographic News, May 9, 2013.

Do you think these "outreach" programs; campaign contributions to elected conservatives, might be a little too much corporate influence over legislative decisions? Are 56% of elective congressional officials (Republicans) suffering a cognitive disconnect concerning scientific data or do they just lack the intellectual capability to process and then reach rational conclusions? Do they all have a very low concentration of GABA?

Homo sapiens are approaching an Event Horizon - a point of no return.

Deforestation

Trees, how many of 'em do we need to look at?"
RONALD REAGAN

Destroying rain forest for economic gain is like burning a Renaissance painting to cook a meal. "
EDWARD O. WILSON

Early humans practiced slash and burn; clearing an area by cutting and burning the vegetation. They would temporarily locate their settlement there until the soil's fertility declined. They would then move on to a more fertile area and repeat the process. That is the time when *Homo sapiens* started the systematic destruction of the planet earth.

Easter Island, located 2,300 miles west of Chile and some 2,500 miles southeast of the Marquesas Islands, measures 14 by 7 miles. It was first visited by Europeans on April 5, 1722, Easter Sunday, by Dutch navigator, Jacob Roggeveen. He estimated the population to be about 2-3000 inhabitants. Archeologists have given estimates that the first inhabitants arrived about 800 AD, however there is some suggestions that they could have arrived as early as 400 AD or as late as 1200 AD. Oral history says the first inhabitants arrived in two large canoes with about 30 men, women and children with provisions that included bananas, taro, sugarcane, paper mulberry, chickens and rats; the rats either as stowaways or brought intentionally as a food source. Their origin is thought to be the Marquesas Islands. Easter Island, at the time of the arrival of the Rapa Nui, as they were known, was a subtropical island populated with at least 21 species of trees that grew up to 50 feet, including the world's largest palm trees, *Paschalococos disperta,* which grew to 65 feet tall with large trunks measuring 36 inches in diameter. There were six species of native land birds. By 1722 most all these plants and birds were extinct.

Nearly 900 giant stone statues, called *moai,* have been found all around the island. They range from 6 to 33 feet tall and weigh up to 86 tons. They were carved to resemble humans, but with over sized heads, long ears and pursed lips on top of thighs, without a mid-trunk. Over the period of approximately 800 years, the population increased to an estimated 15,000. They split into several settlements or tribes. By the 1500's the collapse was very evident. The forests had disappeared, caused by the rats which ate the palm seeds and by man himself as fuel and as the material for their oceangoing canoes. Porpoise, which weigh up to 165 pounds, as well as tuna and other pelagic fish disappeared from their diet, as determined by examination of their middens. Starvation and wars between tribes followed. Without the trees, and becoming over populated the Rapa Nui culture collapsed. The Easter Islanders had no idea what the consequence were to be. I'm sure they had no malicious intent to self destruct. If only they had had cameras, they just might have had a record of the virginal island their ancestors first saw. If only they had practiced rational thought and had been environmentally aware, but obviously they didn't. http://www.smithsonianmag.com/people-places/

So do we, modern *Homo sapiens,* have the rationality, sufficient knowledge and awareness to not follow the path of the Rapa Nui people? Should we take another look at our photo album?

Energy Needs

> *"To truly transform our economy, protect our security, and save our planet from the ravages of climate change, we need to ultimately make clean, renewable energy the profitable kind of energy."*
>
> Barack Obama

Let's be logical and rational and find a solution. As humans, we come upon a problem, we solve the problem. Obviously we need energy. The solution is obvious. We will simply do away with carbon based fuel. We'll rely upon renewable resources. Simple solution, problem solved.

If you have followed the ongoing debate concerning climate change you realize that environmentalists believe that we should switch over to alternative fuels; solar, geothermal, biofuels, wind power, hydroelectric, tides and waves. Continued usage of nuclear energy is debatable.

However the petroleum industry won't keep quiet; and for good reasons. The first reason is that they produce fossil fuel energy and have too much at stake to just abandon this extremely rich source of revenue. The petroleum industry produces millions of jobs; the executives make tons of money and the stockholders, most anyone that has a retirement plan, have a stake in the energy market. A sudden switch away from fossil fuels would create a world wide crisis. The second, equally important reason why switching is problematic is that these alternative sources of energy may not be sufficient to power our needs. Therein lies the conundrum. Is it possible to provide sufficient energy for the entire world's needs without the reliance upon fossil fuel?

How much energy are we using and what will be our future needs? How much of our future needs could renewable energy provide? What would be the downside if we were to make the switch? The huge human concern: what would be the long term costs of *not* switching? Considering how difficult it is to convince not only legislators in Congress, but the general public, is it possible to switch, even to fluorescent light bulbs? People are resistant to change.

The 2008 total yearly world energy supply was 143,851 TWh (terawatt-hour). Converting this number to a personal level, you could use your 'share' by burning 143,000 light bulbs rated at 100 watts, continuously for a year. Of course some of us use more, especially industry and some of us use considerably fewer.

"The answer my friend, is blowin' in the wind"
BOB DYLAN

Present estimates of energy generated today from renewable energy sources range from 16 to 19%, worldwide. Nuclear power generates another 10%. However nuclear power energy production has fallen 4.3% due to safety concerns and disasters. At best, we are only about 1/4 of the way to become fossil fuel independent. The number of solar and wind generators is increasing, quite noticeably in Europe. The downside to switching is, in my opinion rather small compared to the cost if we do nothing. There are a few minor concerns: locating wind farms near population centers presents problems; shadow casting and noise. Bird collisions do happen regardless where they are located. Jobs lost from the petroleum industry will most likely be recovered by new green technologies.

Can the switch be accomplished as long as elections are, to a large part, financed by corporations? I have no answer. Will the general populace embrace green technologies? Yes, as long as the switch won't affect them too greatly economically. There will also be some reluctance to go green by those few who always seem to believe that there is a conspiracy going on. An evil collaboration between the sinister climate scientists and, who knows; the CIA, Big Government, the Liberals. If you were to know any scientists, you would realize that most are independent, analytical and skeptical; they couldn't possibly keep a conspiracy secret as they are always collaborating and sharing data. They are far too busy for such nonsense. Sorry, no evil conspiracy amongst climatologists.

Homo sapiens have not been very good caretakers of our planet. Exploitation rather than long term conservation unfortunately will be our legacy. Deforestation of the Amazon Basin and other forested regions all over the earth is continuing. Our increasing demand for energy supplied by the Petroleum Industry, how we handle industrial waste, unsustainable agriculture, over fishing, human activity such as the Exxon-Valdez accident and nuclear disasters as well as over population *and* the Climate Crisis; these human activities will be duly noted as the legacy of *Homo sapiens.*

There is a canary in the coal mine and he is not looking too happy.

9

Human Constructs - Religion and Politics

Religion

"When the missionaries came to Africa they had the Bible and we had the land. They said 'Let us pray'. We closed our eyes. When we opened them we had the Bible and they had the land"
DESMOND TUTU

WITHIN SCIENCE, VALIDATION is required for a hypothesis to gain acceptance in the scientific community. Normally, validation is achieved by the scientific method of hypothesis, experimental design, empirical evidence, peer review, adversarial review, reproduction of results, conference presentation and journal publication. Science is complicated. To grasp some scientific knowledge requires enormous study and concentration.

Religion appeals to many of the unschooled. Religion requires relatively no expertise nor vast intelligence or scholarly study. Most religious individuals do not study the Bible in any detail. Granted, there are biblical scholars who study the Bible from the viewpoint of history or literature and there are seminary students and preachers that read and take the bible literally. The *Flock*, usually reads passages suggested by their spiritual leader. They never question the authenticity of the Bible. These individuals accept it on faith. The beauty of religion is that it is so simplistic. *Do this or it's hell for you.* Science requires a great deal of study and understanding, background and intelligence. It is not readily accessible to the general public without intense study. All the "miracles" and cures of the past centuries were built upon the science of western civilization. Spiritual enlightenment, the human soul, a vital force, energy fields, all leading to an evolved humanity living in global harmony. Poetically compelling, but these New Age thoughts are well beyond the scope of scientific inquiry. Unfortunately, some individuals believe that the supernatural transcends science.

"I do not find in orthodox Christianity one redeeming feature".
THOMAS JEFFERSON

The Bible has contributed absolutely nothing to creativity and intellectual wisdom. We accept the theories concerning gravity, of light, electromagnetic radiation, theories that help us understand electrons, nuclear power and how the body functions. Surprisingly, slightly more than 50% of residents of The United States of America do not believe in evolution; rather, they believe that evolution is contradicted by their Bible and that man just recently appeared on earth about 10.000 years ago as a creation of God. Dinosaurs are problematic. Faith is the suspension of reason.

The faithful say that evolution lacks direction and purpose. Absolutely true. Evolution does not state that we were created with a purpose; it cannot do this. It's a theory, not a source of philosophic mumbo jumbo. It does not acknowledge either the presence or absence of a god or a creator. God was a concept created by man to give explanations to what is or was unexplainable. The Theory of Evolution has no moral or ethical principles and it makes no judgment of the atrocities of men.

"Religion is what keeps the poor from murdering the rich."
NAPOLEON BONAPARTE

As a metaphor, consider the complexity of a modern automobile to that of religion. Look under the hood of a contemporary auto and you may not recognize any of the components; they are all covered with shrouds. Much like religion. A mechanic schooled in the internal combustion engine does understand how the engine components function and how they are integrated such that the car moves forward. He knows what is under the shrouds and why the car companies place shrouds; to protect the owner from sticking his hand in the fan or onto the battery. The shrouds may also be there to keep the owner from making their own repairs. Shrouds add a bit of mystery and provides a source of revenue for dealerships.

Religion is similarly shrouded; a veil of mystery to prevent the practitioner from too closely examining the tenants of religion. Adam and Eve, Noah and the Ark, water into wine should not be examined.

Science is the intellectual and practical activity encompassing the systematic study of the structure and behavior of the physical and natural world through observation and experiment. Too often we seek simplistic explanations, which may be comforting to some, but lack veracity. If there is but one god and he is omnipotent, why are there approximately 4,200 religions worldwide with about 12 considered major religions. Why is there not just one worldwide religion?

> *"We are a nation that is unenlightened because of religion. I do believe that. I think religion stops people from thinking. I think it justified crazies."*
>
> BILL MAHER

I don't have a clear perception of religious people's idea of heaven or the afterlife. Religious leaders tell us about heaven. I've heard that we will be together again with all our loved ones, at God's feet, if we're fortunate to have not sinned too much. This certainly brings a whole lot of questions to mind. What apparent age are we all? Is Grandmother a young girl? Are we able to communicate with her? Would she know about our life after her passing? Does she have normal bodily functions; has she hunger, does she pee? Would a baby that died always be a baby in heaven; unable to communicate? Who would change the diapers? Is heaven a beautiful garden with flowers (always in bloom) and butterflies? Would there be any mosquitoes? What about the 72 virgins and the eternal erection that Islamic Martyrs believe will be in their future? Why would religious leaders say these questions are unknowable or trite, yet say of our deceased relatives "they are in a better place". How could they possibly know?

I wouldn't state that God doesn't exist. His/her existence is beyond human experience and observation. I would say one can explain the universe, the earth and all life that exists and had existed, without the need for any supernatural cause. Individuals that have "experienced" God or a supernatural energy have not rigorously explored rational explanations for their experiences.

The relevant question: With this world view, is my life better and is it fulfilled? A resounding yes. If one understands that there are rational explanations of what life is, that all life on earth followed well understood evolutionary principals, that this is all there is; that is a fulfilled life.

"You don't need religion to have morals. If you can't determine right from wrong, then you lack empathy, not religion."
ANONYMOUS

If you believe that there is no God, then all your choices depend upon reasoned thought; consideration of all possibilities and accepting their consequences. I'm amazed that most athletes point up to the sky when entering the field or at bat, with the assumption that God will bless them with a home run or whatever. If players from opposing teams offer similar prayers for a favorable outcome, does God make a choice as to which player or team he prefers? We know that's ridiculous. It is often stated that God doesn't play favorites. Then why do athletics pray for positive outcomes? Occasionally your prayer is answered, or are they? To me it's a great comfort to know that no outside supernatural force will affect the outcome. That which affects the outcome can be understood by known scientific forces.

How do we *Homo sapiens* refrain from irrational and speculative ideas that originated from religious views? The scriptures of the Jews, Muslims, Islam, Christians, Hindus or Buddhists give us some moral guidance, but man made laws are the rule of most societies. These rules are sufficient for a productive and peaceful existence.

Religious people are less intelligent than atheists; this is the conclusion of Dr. Miron Zuckerman, University of Rochester. A meta-analysis of 63 studies showed a significant negative association between intelligence and religiosity. He discovered that intelligent children grasp religious ideas earlier, that they are also the first to doubt the truth of religion, and that intelligent students are much less likely to accept orthodox beliefs, and rather less likely to have pro-religious attitudes concluding that perhaps intelligent people have less need, on average, for religious belief and practices. This research titled: "The Relation Between Intelligence and Religiosity" was published in the August 6, 2013, Journal, Personality and Social Psychology Review.

> *"Self-awareness is a trait that not only makes us human but also paradoxically makes us want to be more than merely human. "Science tells us we are merely beasts, but we don't feel like that. We feel like angels trapped inside the bodies of beasts, forever craving transcendence."*
> V.S. Ramachandran, The Tell-Tale Brain: A Neuroscientist's Quest for What makes us Human.

With a nod to Garrison Keillor, here are my answers to *Life's Persistent Questions*:

What's the origin of religion? How is religion practiced as compared to the sacred gospels and how it is misused by some for their agendum and convenience? Why is religion still "practiced". Would we not be better off to discontinue its practice, considering we are living in the 21st century, 300 years post The Age of Enlightenment?

> *It is far better to grasp the universe as it really is than to persist in delusion, however satisfying and reassuring.*
> Carl Sagan

My personal view is that the first human behavior that one might call religious was at the time, in our cognitive development a million or so years ago, when man could comprehend self and ownership, relate to past and future events and developed the facility of curiosity; when people wondered about events relating to themselves. Why is there lightning and earthquakes, why did he die, he was such a good person or what happens to the dead?

There must have been at least one of our ancient ancestors, a resourceful person that first offered explanations for the unexplainable; that was the origin of religion.

That someone, the priest, found a path to obtaining power; power that might even rival the chief's. I assume that intellectual and creative priests went on to offer up even more elaborate explanations a product of their imagination. I would assume that a priest had believers, or followers in such numbers that he might balance the power of the chief. The chief would not offend the priest as the priest might cast a spell; the priest could control the minds of the tribe. The priest couldn't exert too much power as the chief might have him exterminated; the chief could rule by physical strength. These two positions, priest and chief continuously battled for the supreme control over the tribe, (or congregation or nation) from these early times to the present. There are no record of the history of the emergence of religion, as surely this must have happened hundreds of thousand years before recorded time. Pure speculation without evidence, like any good ole religion.

The next question, of which I'm sure the reader could offer some thoughts; what happened? Religion has such lofty ideals, but the practitioners certainly take liberty. Need examples? Brutality and War. It seems that priests are practical. They offer justification and forgiveness for most all bad human behavior; yet bad behavior prevails.

"I do not feel obliged to believe that the same God who has endowed us with sense, reason and intellect has intended us to forgo their use."
GALILEO GALILEI

The Age of Enlightenment can be traced to 17th and 18th century Europe and on to the American colonies. It was a challenge to faith, tradition, superstition and the intolerance and abuses of power by the church and state. Its purpose was to reform society by reason and the scientific method. Early proponents were Spinoza, John Locke, Voltaire and Isaac Newton. *The Age of Enlightenment* greatly influenced American colonists Ben Franklin and Thomas Jefferson as reflected in the Declaration of Independence and the Bill of Rights.

Why, in the 21st century does religion still exist? Certainly, religion does bring comfort to many in times of distress. When scientific or reasoned answers to questions are unsatisfying to some individuals, religion often offers alternative explanations as well as comfort. Religious congregations practice compassion to many of the unfortunate. Food and clothing banks are common endeavors of religious groups. There are numerous non-religious groups that serve the unfortunate as well. Good Will, the United Way and the Red Cross along with religious groups step up in times of disasters. Compassion and empathy is a very endearing human trait. What I find disturbing is when religious dogma influences politics and when religious missionary groups link compassion with recruitment.

Here is an example shared by a few. Alan, a good friend from my university days would often attend Catholic Mass; however he professed to be an atheist. The reason for this apparent contradiction was that he was an *Aesthetic Catholic.* He enjoyed the ceremony, the music, the stained glass and the stillness of the great cathedrals; he found comfort and solitude. I could understand his position. He took what suited him and dismissed the rest.

Thanksgiving is a day set aside to give thanks for all that we have. It is not a day to wish for more.

Politics

> *"One of the penalties for refusing to participate in politics is that you end up being governed by your inferiors."*
>
> PLATO

In 1997, Carl Sagan, was interviewed by Charlie Rose. Sagan contended that power and ignorance should be of great concern. *"We don't run the government, the government runs us... We live in the age of science and technology and few politicians have the education to understand either... Science is more than a body of knowledge, it's a way of thinking".*

Politics refers to achieving and exercising positions of governance; organized control over a human community, particularly a state. It can also refer to a particular set of political beliefs or principles. Aristotle's treatise on the *"Affairs of the Cities"* is cited as an early reference to political organizing.

In tribal situations, tens to hundreds of thousands of years ago, conservative values might have been selfishly hoarding food. Selfishness may be self defeating. It's likely that the selfish person would be shunned, otherwise his behavior could jeopardize the tribe. At times one must be selfish to some degree or you and your genome won't survive, for example, obtaining sufficient food. One argument that a liberal philosophy may be better for humanity is that as tribal animals; it got us to where we are now.

We are all affected by politics and we are involved in politics either actively or passively. Few are dispassionate. Most belong to or feel associated with a political group. It's as if we belong to a tribe. During election season we fly their colors. Comparing one's political party to a tribe is not too far off the mark. Everyone dislikes negative ads, but they continue to be used because they effectively coalesce their base supporters; they create doubt and fear of the alternative candidate.

Little is known about the biology of political ideology; specifically the degree of any genetic basis for our political persuasion. A recent scientific paper addresses this issue.

A Genome-Wide Analysis of Liberal and Conservative Political Attitudes, Peter K. Hatemi, et.al. The Journal of Politics, January 14, 2011. *"Here, we present the first genome-wide analysis of Conservative-Liberal attitudes from a sample of 13,000 respondents whose DNA was collected in conjunction with a 50-item sociopolitical attitude questionnaire. Several significant linkage peaks were identified and potential candidate genes discussed. ....no gene is acting directly to determine our political views–there is no "liberal" or "conservative" gene–but there might be a combination of genes acting together that somehow predispose us to have particular politics, presumably through their role in influencing our brains and thus our personalities or social behaviors."*

Our political viewpoints are often those of our parents and our close and admired friends. Our life experiences and the messages from political think tanks and advocacy groups temper our views. We seem to need simple, easy to comprehend messages without complexity or intellectual burden. Rationality should prevail; unfortunately, it often does not. Critical analysis of most any political candidate or proposition would most likely reveal both positive and negative attributes. Propositions are placed on ballots by either legislators or advocacy groups to advance their interests and hopefully the interests of their constituents. Once the candidate announces his candidacy or a proposition is on the ballot, political consultants are hired, the TV ads appear, back to back, endlessly. Too much money is at stake.

Think Tanks or Advocacy Groups are devoted to articulating political views; creating talking points, as well as influencing public policy. These think tanks are large and very well funded and have enormous influence.

Examples of these groups:

The Heritage Foundation is an American conservative think tank. Their stated mission is formulate and promote conservative public policies.

The Cato Institute is an American libertarian think tank founded by Charles Koch.

The Center for American Progress is a progressive public policy research and advocacy organization. It presents the liberal perspective.

The Brookings Institution conducts research in the social sciences, governance and domestic and global economic policies. It is politically independent.

> *"The only difference between compassionate conservatism and conservatism is that under compassionate conservatism they tell you they're not going to help you but they're really sorry about it."*
>
> TONY BLAIR

Compassionate Conservatism was the campaign slogan of George W. Bush. The basis tenants, the core values of the conservatives' position is self interest; pay little or no tax and have limited government. Limiting government primarily to defense, is a core value for two reasons. It's a whole lot cheaper if we were to eliminate many governmental departments and agencies such as The Environmental Protection Agency, the Department of Education and The National Endowment for the Arts. These agencies and department have been highlighted for elimination by conservatives; the EPA to eliminate regulations protecting the environment and Education which restricts religious teachings in public schools. Just a very minor First Amendment problems. Concerning the NEA; they just don't like liberals. Conservatives argue that fewer governmental restrictions would stimulate creativity and innovation. All this for greater wealth for the nation and the individual. Governmental oversight stifles growth. Conservatives take a short time frame as opposed to long term view. Advocates for the conservative agenda say that America would be a better and freer nation if we were to follow conservative principles. They see little need for food stamp programs, governmental health care or the need for inspectors that might identify and prevent pollution of our water resources or prevent contamination of our food processing. Self-regulation is sufficient. Conservatives say that governmental departments that regulate and police many activities should be outsourced or eliminated. Cost cutting measures that benefit corporations and their investors short term are rarely considered in long term costs and benefits in their analysis. Over regulation surely stifles innovation but any system, biological or physical, needs to be regulated and kept within acceptable parameters, or it will self destruct. We have conservatives worried that we overspend, over protect, over regulate, over think, over analyze and that there are too many leftwing liberals, intellectuals, artists, poets and free thinkers destroying the American Way of Life.

Some conservatives certainly do favor certain laws; drug enforcement, mandatory sentencing, Defense of Marriage laws, laws that dictate morality and "voter fraud" laws which have resulted in one dozen actual prosecuted cases over the last decade, nationwide. They do favor some government spending for more prisons, but not higher education; let the banks take care of student loans. Conservatives can be at times compassionate. Viewing the society pages of newspapers, one sees photographs of galas and society balls with the wealthy socialites in attendance. Most certainly these events do benefit honorable charities.

Disseminating information to other tribe members is a behavioral trait that goes back to tribal councils. Today, it's the media; a source to spread information that is hardly completely unbiased. News is gathered and produced by humans, all of whom have experiences that give a bias; journalists and their editors and the editor's board of directors all have some sort of bias. The First Amendment to the United States Constitution: *Congress shall make no law respecting an establishment of religion, or prohibiting the free exercise thereof; or abridging the freedom of speech, or of the press; or the right of the people peaceably to assemble, and to petition the Government for a redress of grievances.*

Whereas we do have freedom of speech, that speech does not necessarily imply that it is the truth or the whole truth.

Serious investigations of political positions is beyond the interest of too many people. Ignorance of science is to blame for some of our flawed policies. The news media, out of realistic financial considerations, make conscientious decisions regarding the constituency they serve, the content of the news; which story, and which candidate is covered. Given these considerations, the news is slanted yet it greatly influences our thinking. Sometimes it results in *Public Bamboozlement.*

It is nearly Impossible to change a tribe member's views, even when new information goes against their closely held beliefs, even if it's contrary to logic or their best interest. Change can be threatening to the peace and harmony of the tribe. If we had the sensibility and talent of Mr. Spock, logic and rationality would prevail. *Homo sapiens* do not have this mental capacity.

George W. Bush ran commercials mocking Al Gore saying he claims to have invented the Internet. Therefore claimed Bush, Gore is a liar and he can't be trusted. In a March 1999 interview with Wolf Blitzer on CNN, Al Gore said, *"During my service in the United States Congress, I took the initiative in creating the Internet. I took the initiative in moving forward a whole range of initiatives that have proven to be important to our country's economic growth and environmental protection, improvements in our educational system."*

Cross-tabulation analysis is a system that identifies the popular and compelling political arguments and how to frame the argument. Political consultants use these analyses to insure that the voter will act "appropriately" on those key messages. Knowing which messages are compelling and how to frame the message has the power to change attitudes and influence voting behavior. This can make the difference between winning and losing.

"The intellect is always fooled by the heart".
FRANCOIS DE LA ROCHEFOUCAULD

Wedge issues are social issues that polarize people, one of the tools of political action groups. Killing fetuses versus taking away the reproductive rights of women are emotional wedge issues used by political operatives to coalesce their constituents. Each group fights back; antiabortionists label themselves as "pro-life" while pro-abortion groups label themselves as "pro-choice". Ever noticed that Pro-life advocates are often pro-Death Penalty? Climate change has unfortunately become a wedge issue; liberal conspirators versus fossil fuel advocates.

Frank Luntz is a political consultant for the Republican Party. He is a popular commentator and guest on *Fox News.* He runs focus groups which test words and language that help conservative candidates better express a view acceptable to the target audience. Lutz tests words and phrases on focus groups to gage their emotional effectiveness. Interviewed on PBS Frontline, March 23, 2007, Lutz said *"80 percent of our life is emotion, and only 20 percent is intellect. I am much more interested in how you feel than how you think."* He is very clever with language and understands human behavior; taking complex issues, simplifying and modifying these issues to either take on a positive spin or create fear. One might consider Lutz to be a master of *Hoodwinking and Duping.*

Conservatives and Capitalism

"How can you be content to be in the world like tulips in a garden, to make a fine show and be good for nothing."
MARY ASTELL

It is my personal view that *Homo sapiens* remain tribal. Two tribes, the conservatives that champion capitalism and the other tribe, the liberals that tend to have socialistic ideals. Over simplistic, yes, but it seems to me, that especially in today's environment with political wars between the two political parties, these two nearly opposite positions are relevant and help in our examination of just what we are, and why.

The conservative trait could be characterized as having a selfish nature; always looking out for themselves; looking for the bargain, tax avoidance and accumulating wealth. Conservatives are sober, modest and cautious. They hold as certain that if we live as conservatives, we increase the probability that our genes will be passed onto the next generation. And we will have greater freedom. They abhor socialism and contend that it is forced or involuntary cooperation.

"Regarding the current political debate over government tax and spending issues, there are several points on which all conservatives agree. First, the federal government has grown way too large and is engaged in too many activities that transcend constitutional boundaries. Second, in this unrestrained role, the government is spending way too much money and running up way too large of deficits. Third, this overspending and deficit irresponsibility threaten not only the very integrity and authority of government, but the foundation and health of the American economy."
PATRICK GARRY, RENEWAMERICA, DECEMBER 16, 2011

"The forces of a capitalist society, if left unchecked, tend to make the rich richer and the poor poorer". Jawaharlal Nehru, 1958

"Capitalism is a big problem, because with capitalism you're just going to keep buying and selling things until there's nothing else to buy and sell, which means gobbling up the planet."
ALICEWALKER

Capitalism is an economic system in which a country's trade and industry are controlled by private owners and goods and services produced are sold for profit in a market economy. The history of Capitalism has been traced back to the 9th century in the Islamic world. Sharia, or Islamic law deals with many moral and religious topics as well as systems of politics and economics. Sharia encourages charity and discourages usury on loans.

A merchant form of capitalism started in the 12th century Europe and by the 16th century, a recognizable form was active in The Netherlands, with the beginnings of full time stock exchanges. Remembered from this era was the speculative economic tulip market. From November 12, 1636 to February 3, 1637, the price of some single tulip bulbs soared to ten times the annual wage of a skilled worker. On May 1, the same year, the market collapsed. This *Tulip Mania* is generally considered the first recorded speculative bubble.

Europeans capitalized on this early form of capitalism by building even larger ships to bring back treasures from the new world, Africa, Asia and most anywhere where they traded their religion and manufactured goods for new resources. Vast intercontinental trading brought great wealth to the seagoing merchants.

Greater wealth, in part, brought *The Industrial Revolution.* The industrial leaders increased their wealth while the working class was at the mercy of those controlling the resources. What emerged was a three class system; a very small exclusive wealthy class, the merchant class and the uneducated working class. Wealth equals power, and the separation between classes increased steadily. Now, many, if not most, would consider capitalism as good, a system that promotes freedom and the good life. The goods available to us now are many; flat-screen TVs, smart phones and fast cars. It's been a smashing success.

Consider that today, with a USA wealth of 54 trillion dollars; the top one percent of Americans have 40% of the wealth and own 50% of all stocks, bonds and mutual funds. The bottom 80% has 7% of the wealth. The bottom 50% of Americans own 0.5% of stocks, bond and mutual funds; they are just scraping by. *The Trickle Down* theory in practice; gives tax breaks to the wealthy as they are the "Job Creators". They will create jobs and we all will be better off. Here are some facts. In 1995, the *Millionaires Effective Tax Rate* was 30.4%. In 2009 with the Bush tax cuts in effect, the millionaires tax rate dropped to 22.4 %. Unemployment in 1995 was 5.6 %. However, the 14 years of lower tax rates for the rich resulted in an *increase* in unemployment to 9.3%. Obviously there were many factors to the joblessness but tax breaks for the wealthy did result in greater unemployment; the exact opposite that the Republicans promised. Information by Nick Hanauer, from a *banned* TED talk labelled "Too politically controversial", 2012. It is rumored that TED did not want to offend the wealthy attendees.

Dacher Keltner, a professor of psychology at Berkeley, "found that the poor, compared with the wealthy, have keenly attuned interpersonal attention in all directions. Generally, those with the most power in society seem to pay particularly little attention to those with the least power. In politics, readily dismissing inconvenient people can easily extend to dismissing inconvenient truths about them. The insistence by some House Republicans in Congress on cutting financing for food stamps and impeding the implementation of Obamacare, ... may stem in part from the empathy gap".

http://opinionator.blogs.nytimes.com/2013/10/05/rich-people-just-care-less/?_r=0

In 1950, executives were paid about 20 times the wages of their workers. Now the average executive receives 240 times that of their average workers. Wages for the average worker has barely increased compared to executive's compensation which has skyrocketed. http://www.bloomberg.com, April 29, 2013. Perhaps today's CEO's are working 12 times more hours per day that they did 60 years ago. That equates to working 96 hours per day.

Today, in our capitalistic system of commerce, corporations are consolidating, in essence eliminating their competition and shipping their manufacturing overseas to lower their cost of production. Jobs are eliminated. Automation is clearly a job cutting 'measure'. Large stockholders and corporate executives; the top one percent, are joyful as profits soar and their dividends increase. Corporate leaders are even more joyful as their compensations have increased enormously. The jobless can always go on "Family Assistance", that is, until their benefits run out. Capitalism as an economic system is based on perpetual growth, with the inevitable depletion on the world's natural resources. Long term it is unsustainable. Did humans adopt a better way of life with capitalism? A few certainly did.

One persistent attitude attributed to capitalism is that this form of commerce promotes motivation, the driving force for a vibrant economy.

"Socialism is unsustainable as it destroys the motivation to work".

There is some truth to this. With innovation comes new and improved goods. Rewards are given to the innovators and producers. The economy grows.

The downside to this is that often more jobs are lost than gained. Competition between corporations becomes fierce, often with the industry laggers resorting to corrupt practices; dumping waste into a water source as a cheaper method of disposal. When industry leaders' profits increase, we often see their profits funneled to Washington lobbyists "asking" legislators to decrease their client's taxes. As profits increase, lobbying expenses follow.

"The Sunlight Foundation, a watchdog group advocating for government transparency, analyzed the 200 largest U.S. companies, ranked by 2010 pre-tax income, and found those that spent the most on lobbying between 2007 and 2009 had lower 2010 tax rates than what they paid in 2007".

http://abcnews.go.com/Business/exxon-mobil-verizon-companies-spent-lobbying-lower-tax/story?id=16162792

With the debt ceiling and fiscal debates forever ongoing; as taxes are lowered and personal incomes increase for the top economic group, isn't it obvious what a solution could be? Are not stockholders partly to blame, with their expectations of higher returns, firing executives that fail to meet high expectations?

Liberals and Socialism

The liberal traits of man could be characterized as tolerant, open and broad minded, progressive, enlightened, flexible, philanthropic, and benevolent, looking out for the needs of the whole tribe. If we and the rest of the tribe have this trait, the tribe is stronger long term. When *hominins* moved out onto the grasslands, there were the game animals to hunt down. Great skill and tribal cooperation was needed to capture and butcher these food resources. Only the swift and cunning could accomplish this. Tribes without the skills of organization and cooperation did not survive.

<u>Liberal Accomplishments</u>

Medicare
Social Security
Securities and Exchange Commission
Federal Reserve

Food and Drug Administration
National Park Service
Federal School Lunch Program
Food Stamps
Voting Rights Act
Equal Access to Public Accommodations
Collective Bargaining
Fair Labor Standards
Clean Air Act
Clean Water Act
Equal Rights for Women
Affordable Care Act

"Every one of these efforts, which strengthened our democracy and the quality of life in America, began as a liberal initiative contested by conservatives."
GEORGE McGOVERN, 2004, THE ESSENTIAL AMERICA.

A libertarian might think that these governmental programs are unnecessary and impede our individual freedom; efforts by the liberals to level the playing field; a socialist money grab, a redistribution of wealth at the expense of the hard working wage earners; a social engineering program.

"I believe in a relatively equal society, supported by institutions that limit extremes of wealth and poverty. I believe in democracy, civil liberties, and the rule of law. That makes me a liberal, and I'm proud of it."
PAUL KRUGMAN

"Capitalism is the worst enemy of humanity. Capitalism and the senseless development of unlimited industrialization are what destroy the environment,"
EVO MORALES, PRESIDENT OF BOLIVIA

A socialist economic system consists of a system of production and distribution organized to directly satisfy economic demands and human needs, so that goods and services are produced directly for use instead of for private profit driven by the accumulation of capital.

The Spanish conquest of the Inca empire began in 1524, and was mostly completed by 1533 with the defeat of the Incas of Bolivia. The Bolivian inhabitants were forced into slavery and were used mercilessly to extract huge amounts of silver; 41,000 metric tons of pure silver were mined from 1556 to 1783. The Spanish reign lasted 300 years.

Bolivia has struggled through periods of dictatorship, political instability and economic woes. There were coup d'état, counter-coups, and caretaker governments. Bolivia was named for Simon Bolivar on August 6, 1825. He was a military and political leader who played a key role in the struggle for independence from the Spanish Empire.

During the early 20th century there has been a succession of Bolivian governments controlled by the economic and social elite following laissez-faire capitalist policies. The CIA had been active in providing finances and training to the Bolivian military dictatorship in 1960s. The revolutionary leader Che Guevara was killed by a team of CIA officers and members of the Bolivian Army on October 9, 1967, in Bolivia.

During much of the 1980s and 90s, international organizations such as the World Bank pushed Bolivia to privatize businesses held by the state. The World Bank was following ideas of the economic *Shock Theory*, a free market theory proposed by Nobel laureate Milton Friedman and then Harvard University economist Jeffery Sachs. Under this policy, public utilities and services such as water, petroleum and mining were sold to private companies in the hope that international investment and a capitalist model would jump-start chronically impoverished Bolivia. This measure was used to cut hyperinflation from an estimated 14,000% to a single digit within a period of 6 weeks. More broadly, Sachs is credited with having engineered the restructuring of the Bolivian state and the dismantling of the state-capitalist model that had prevailed in the country since the 1952 Revolution. Unintended consequences of these policies included fallen wages by 40%, labor unrest and governmental kidnappings of union leaders. Greater detail about this policy can be found in Naomi Klein's excellent book The Shock Doctrine: The Rise of Disaster Capitalism, 2007.

Vivir Bien

Evo Morales was the first indigenous President of Bolivia, elected to office in 2005 with 53% of the vote. Evo Morales' political philosophy can be summarized by the phrase, *vivir bien*, which literally means "living well," but its meaning in Bolivia is closer to "living in the right way" or "living appropriately, so that others may also live."

When Morales was elected, he responded by forcing companies to renegotiate oil and gas contracts. That resulted in significantly increased income for the government. He instituted social programs that aided the elderly, students and mothers with young children. His platform was to reclaim the country's natural resources, protecting its biodiversity and water resources, respecting and strengthening the indigenous land ownership rights of the country's impoverished majority.

His argument was that the western world was based on material accumulation, and this led to economic policies that were destroying the planet. Rather than trying to "live better," he said our goal should be to "live well." *"Capitalism has created a civilization that is wasteful, consumerist, exclusive, clientelist, a generator of opulence and misery. That is the pattern of life, production and consumption that we urgently need to transform"*. In 2009, Morales was reelected with a landslide majority, polling 64%; an increase over his 54% polling four years earlier.

http://climateandcapitalism.com/2013/01/15/evo-morales-ten-commandments-against-capitalism-for-life-and-humanity/

Many New Testament scholars say that Jesus Christ was a socialist; he performed acts that most would identify as socialistic. He healed the sick and fed the poor, presumedly without renumeration. Today, many would consider that socialism is a very nasty word. We fling it around as we did the word Communist 60 years ago. Of the many epithets used to describe President Obama, is that he is a Socialist, but not in a flattering manner.

By numerous polls, Denmark as been rated as the happiest country in the world; where their citizens are the most content. Denmark along with other Scandinavian countries have high taxation but with medical and educational benefits beyond ours. The overall tax burden (sum of all taxes, as a percentage of GDP) is estimated to be 46% in 2011. Denmark has the world's lowest level of income inequality, according to the World Bank, which also ranks Denmark as the easiest place in Europe to do business. Denmark also has the world's highest minimum wage as well as having one of the world's highest per capita income. It also has the fourth highest ratio of individuals with advanced degrees. All college and university education in Denmark is free of charges; there are no tuition fees to enroll in courses. Along with Sweden and Norway, Denmark has a universal health care system, financed by taxes and not by social contributions. On September 6, 2012, Denmark launched the biggest wind turbine in the world, and will add four more over the next four years. Additionally, Denmark's intra-structure is well maintained. Most conservatives consider Denmark to be a Socialist State.

10

Conservatives Versus Liberals

"Liars and panderers in government would have a much harder time if so many people didn't insist on their right to remain ignorant and blindly agreeable."
BILL MAHER

THERE IS AN ongoing battle between conservatives and liberals. Congress is so discombobulated as to be nonfunctional. What should be the role of government? To what extent should we be a capitalistic society? Remember what Ronald Reagan said: *"The worst nine words you may hear is that 'I'm from the government and I'm here to help"*.

Really?

Consider these 48 words: *"Due to Federal budget cuts, Head Start and Food Stamp programs, The Center for Disease Control, Food Safety agencies, The Departments of Health and Human Services, Education, the EPA, NEA, NSF are dissolved. However, congressional members and their staff as well as The Department of Defense are unaffected"*.

My best nine words you might (or might not) hear: *One hundred Wall Street manipulators have gone to jail.*

Is government too big? How big is too big? What Ronald Reagan implied is that out-sourcing is better than having government providing services and that the government should not provide social services. He believed that government was needed for defense, but not much more. Out-sourcing does provide services for the government and has done so for decades. However, there are problems. Governmental contracts usually go to the lowest bidder or to corporations with the largest lobbying funding. That does not necessarily mean there will be savings. To win the bid, corporations either need to be extremely efficient, or take short cuts; which might be costing the government more than expected to correct defects.

A great deal of the intelligence gathering and analysis is out-sourced. Remember Edward Snowden. He received high security clearance from out-sourced contractors. There were cost overruns and misbehavior by the outsourced contractors during the Iraqi War. The Affordable Health Care website was poorly done, again by out-sourced contractors. These are just three examples of problems when the lowest bidder does governmental work. When the government is as huge as it is, there tends to be some bad behavior, slackers and sloppy performances. Corporations have similar troubles as well; they're motivated by profits rather than by patriotism. I think that 99% of people work diligently and have good ethics, but a few, either in government or in the private sector take advantage of "the system".

Can the free-market and for profit corporations save us? One of the most meaningful functions of government is to govern: control, influence, or regulate. Certainly we should apply good principles of governance to dictate what humanity needs to survive. Capitalism seems to not pay attention to this concept when laws are circumvented as a means to increase profits for corporations, their CEO's and stockholders. Profits and return on investments are paramount for these folks. It is difficult to decide whether government or markets work better in every circumstance. All systems require governors. Any system, biological, societal or mechanical, without governance fails. There always seems to be an ongoing battle between the schemers and scammers versus the regulators. When competition between corporations is fierce, with few exemptions, there will be shenanigans. Regulations are devised to alleviate this.

Charitable Giving

"No one has ever become poor by giving."
ANNE FRANK, DIARY OF ANNE FRANK

There have been several studies that examine who are the givers in the U.S. My conservative friends are certain that it is the wealthy that are the ones making significant charitable gifts. In one sense they are correct, but only in terms of the most money given. Comparing giving with their actual annual income, it is the individual in the lower income group that is the most generous. In 2001, the Independent Sector, a nonprofit organization focused on charitable giving, found that those with a household income of less than $25,000 contributed 4.2 %. Households with incomes in excess of $75,000 contributed 2.7 %. http://www.cpanda.org/pdfs/gv/GV01Report.pdf

A more recent study conducted by the Chronicle of Philanthropy, using tax deduction data showed that households earning between $50,000 and $75,000 year give an average of 7.6 percent of their discretionary income to charity. That compares to 4.2 percent for people who make $100,000 or more. In some of the wealthiest neighborhoods, with a large share of people making $200,000 or more a year, the average giving rate was 2.8 percent. http://www.cnbc.com/id/48725147 20 Aug 20, 2012

Another study in 2011 found that Americans with earning in the top 20 percent contributed 1.3 percent of their income to charity by comparison to those in the bottom 20 percent who donated 3.2 percent of their income; that would be 2 1/2 times greater. The relative generosity of lower-income Americans is accentuated by the fact that, unlike middle-class and wealthy donors, most of them cannot take advantage of the charitable tax deduction, because they do not itemize deductions on their income-tax returns. Ken Stern, The Atlantic, April 2013

Taxes

"Last year my federal tax bill — the income tax I paid, as well as payroll taxes paid by me and on my behalf — was $6,938,744. That sounds like a lot of money. But what I paid was only 17.4 percent of my taxable income — and that's actually a lower percentage than was paid by any of the other 20 people in our office. Their tax burdens ranged from 33 percent to 41 percent and averaged 36 percent."

WARREN E. BUFFETT, AN OP-ED EDITORIAL *"STOP CODDLING THE SUPER-RICH"*, NEW YORK TIMES, AUGUST 14, 2011

How Low Are U.S. Taxes Compared to Other Countries? Derek Thompson, January 14, 2013, The Atlantic. *"The U.S. comes in at 55th out of 114 other Organization for Economic Co-operation and Development, (OECD) countries in a graph from the Tax Policy Center. We're at the bottom of the stack, 25 percent below the average." Denmark has the highest at about 47%, the OECD is at 36.2%, the USA is at 27.3% and Mexico the lowest at about 22%."*

The 2013 U.S. Federal Tax Code is 73,954 pages. One reason for its length: legislators expanding the pages to insure that their clients; corporations and special interests, obtain exemptions, i.e., loop holes to lower taxes.

Social Security and Medicare are presently unsustainable, without raising taxes. Why not raise taxes?

Raising taxes to 39.6 percent on the rich would yield around $40 billion to $45 billion in added tax revenue in the first year. Robert Frank, CNBC Reporter and Editor.

"Taxes were far higher on top incomes in the three decades after World War II than they've been since. And the distribution of income was far more equal. Yet the American economy grew faster in those years than it's grown since tax rates were slashed in 1981. This wasn't a post-war aberration. Bill Clinton raised taxes on the wealthy in the 1990s, and the economy produced faster job growth and higher wages than it did after George W. Bush slashed taxes on the rich in his first term.

If you need more evidence, consider modern Germany, where taxes on the wealthy are much higher than they are here and the distribution of income is far more equal. But Germany's average annual growth has been faster than that in the United States."
ROBERT REICH

"Nothing riles Americans quite like taxes.... And when it comes to tax avoidance — the legal means of minimizing one's tax burden, not to be confused with its illegal cousin, tax evasion — a growing chorus of critics say high tax rates are to blame, and an overly complex tax code isn't helping. The emerging point of view: The higher tax rates get, the more people will try to figure out ways to stop paying them."
FOX BUSINESS, MAY 13, 2011.

Tax avoidance is a legal method to reduce the amount of tax one owes, such as claiming the permissible deductions and credits, contributing to employer-sponsored retirement plans and or purchasing municipal bonds. Tax havens are jurisdictions, states or countries, where some taxes are levied at a low or zero rate. Some corporations and individuals establish shell subsidiaries in tax havens as a tax avoidance strategy. Tax evasion is the term for efforts by individuals, corporations and trusts to evade taxes by illegal means.

Tax avoidance may be legal, but is it ethical? A patriot is an individual that is devoted to and vigorous supports their country. Is it patriotic to avoid taxes? We feel it is the responsibility of government to provide services that are essential for this country; roads and bridges, the military, food safety, literally hundreds of services. The services are paid for by taxes. How patriotic are individuals that avoid taxes, even legally? Do the tax avoiders simply lack empathy for their country, every April 15th?

"Taxes should hurt", Ronald Reagan, 1971, although he avoided paying State of California income tax. Daytona Beach Morning Journal, May 8, 1971.

"Taxes are the price we pay for a civilized society."
OLIVER WENDELL HOLMES

U.S. Debt

"It took the national debt two hundred years to reach $1 trillion. Supply Side Economics quadrupled the national debt to over $4 trillion in twelve years (1980-1992) under the Republicans. Bill Clinton actually paid down the national debt. How did he do it? He raised taxes. It produced the longest sustained economic expansion in U.S. History."

ED SCHULTZ

The deficit is the difference between the money Government takes in, called receipts, and what the Government spends, called outlays, each year. The National Debt is the result of the federal government borrowing money to cover years and years of budget deficits.

The US National Debt is $17 trillion dollars and increasing. The individual citizen's responsibility equates to $54,000. The U.S. Federal spending is $3.5 trillion and decreasing. http://www.usdebtclock.org, There is the debt held privately; by outside governments, individual investors, corporations and foreign government. This amount accounts for about 12 trillion dollars (73%) of the National debt. $5 trillion of the public debt is owned by foreign investors, with People's Republic of China and Japan owning $1.1 trillion each. The remainder of the National Debt, 4.9 trillion dollars (29%), is non-marketable Treasuries securities such as Social Security Trust Fund. Public debt increases when government spends and decreases when government receives monies such as taxes.

Everyone agrees that the debt should come down. The disagreement concerns how to accomplish this. The abbreviated answer of the conservatives is to decrease expenditures. Specifics are varied and are often not specific, but shrink the size of government is their general response; abolish many regulatory agencies and public services. The Defense Department's budget should remain intact. The Liberal's approach to solving the national debt: temporarily increase spending; creating jobs that repair our infrastructure, support green technologies, make higher education affordable, decrease military expenses, decrease healthcare costs with universal healthcare and reform the tax code; increase taxation of the rich to the level of the Eisenhower era.

To my dismay, the financial crisis debate is overshadowing the climate crisis.

If climate change is real and there is a crisis approaching, which policies better address this issue? As a nation we are divided down the middle.

I surmise that, as we are *Homo sapiens*, we will muddle along until the climate crisis affect sufficient numbers as to awaken the populace to respond appropriately.

Public Art

"If I could say it in words there would be no reason to paint."
EDWARD HOPPER

The National Endowment for the Arts, was created by an act of the U.S. Congress in 1965 as an independent agency of the federal government. *"dedicated to supporting excellence in the arts, both new and established; bringing the arts to all Americans; and providing leadership in arts education"*. Since its inception, the NEA has awarded more than 140,000 grants, including early support for the Vietnam Veterans Memorial design competition, the Sundance Film Festival, Spoleto Festival USA, PBS's Great Performances series, and the American Film Institute. For more than four decades, the Arts Endowment has encouraged creativity through support of performances, exhibitions, festivals, artist residencies, and other arts projects throughout the country. In partnership with the state and jurisdictional arts agencies and regional arts organizations, the National Endowment for the Arts provides federal support for projects that benefit local communities. http://www.nea.gov

"We believe strongly that the arts aren't somehow an 'extra' part of our national life, but instead we feel that the arts are at the heart of our national life. It is through our music, our literature, our art, drama and dance that we tell the story of our past and we express our hopes for the future. Our artists challenge our assumptions in ways that

many cannot and do not. They expand our understandings, and push us to view our world in new and very unexpected ways...That is the power of the arts -- to remind us of what we each have to offer, and what we all have in common; to help us understand our history and imagine our future; to give us hope in the moments of struggle; and to bring us together when nothing else will. That is what we celebrate here today."

MICHELLE OBAMA, PITTSBURGH CREATIVE & PERFORMING ARTS SCHOOL, SEPTEMBER 25, 2009.

Since its conception there have been numerous conservative attacks aiming to abolish the NEA. Ronald Reagan attempted to abolish the NEA, but was persuaded not to do such by his conservative friends in Hollywood. A period in the late 80's and 90's witnessed abolishment attempts by Pat Robertson, Dick Armey, Pat Buchanan and Donald Wildmon of the American Family Association. Newt Gingrich attempted to eliminate not only the NEA but also the National Endowment for the Humanities and the Corporation for Public Broadcasting. The artists that most offended these people include Andres Serrano, Karen Finley and Robert Mapplethorpe. In 1990, the act governing the U.S. National Endowment for the Arts was amended requiring that the judges of grant applications should take into consideration "*general standards of decency and respect for the diverse beliefs and values of the America public*". The US Supreme Court found the provision to be constitutional.

Entartete Kunst, was the title of an exhibition produced by the Nazi regime in Munich, Germany in 1937. The English translation is *Degenerate Art*, a term used by the Nazis to describe all modern art which was banned on the grounds that it was un-German or Jewish Bolshevist in nature.

The paintings in the *Degenerate Art* exhibition were modernist artworks displayed in a chaotic manner accompanied by disparaging labels. The purpose of their exhibition was to inflame public opinion.

These "degenerate" artworks were in opposition to the regime's insistence that art should exalt Nazi ideals; racial purity, militarism and obedience. During that Nazi period, over 5,000 artworks were seized including works by Nolde, Heckel, Kirchner, Beckmann, Archipenko, Chagall, Ensor, Matisse, Picasso and van Gogh. Artists identified as "degenerate" by the Nazis were subjected to sanctions; dismissal from teaching positions, forbidden to produce, exhibit or sell their art.

The August 20, 2013, issue of the New York Times reported that the House Appropriations Committee has cut the budget of both The National Endowment of the Arts and The National Endowment for the Humanities by one half. The present financing levels are about $155 million each; which represents 0.44 percent of the federal government's budget. Over the last 40 years, the NEA has survived a dozen conservative onslaughts in Congress attempting to dissolve it completely. http://www.nytimes.com/2013/08/20/opinion/trifling-with-the-arts-and-humanities.html

Nick Gillespie, a libertarian American journalist, in the Economist, August 29, 2012, argues that governmental support of specific institutions or individuals is in no way necessary or sufficient for the production of "art" (his quote marks). His second objection is that *"governments everywhere are dead broke."* Further: *"Forced funding of the arts—in whatever trivial amounts and indirect ways—implicates citizens in culture they might openly despise or blissfully ignore. And such mandatory tithing effectively turns creators and institutions lucky enough to win momentary favor from bureaucrats into either well-trained dogs or witting instruments of the powerful and well-connected. Independence works quite well for churches and the press. It works even more wonderfully in the arts."*

So Nick Gillespie, would you consider The Vietnam Veterans Memorial, designed by American architect Maya Lin a waste of federal money? So simple, so elegant. Public and private funding supported The Lincoln Memorial, as well.

> *"It seems that some members of Congress fear the marketplace of ideas, artistic expression and creative innovation precisely because they can't control them. At worst that's a form of fascistic thinking, and reason enough in my mind to support the NEA. At very best, it's using personal values to assess the arts, by which some members of Congress confuse personal morality with public policy. Even more, the NEA funnels 50 percent of its money directly to state arts agencies (by congressional mandate), thereby allowing local standards and selection criteria to prevail (I'm not sure everyone in Congress understands this part). Also, the NEA primes the pump for*

private giving to the arts by individuals, foundations and corporations in amounts which dwarf the NEA's own budget by thousands of times"
JONATHAN ABARBANEL, DEPT. OF THEATER, UNIVERSITY OF ILLINOIS AT CHICAGO. AUGUST 16, 2011

Funding Public Artworks is a contentious topic. Artists, essentially a liberal crowd, Humanists and Liberals, believe that there is a need for public support of the arts; an expression of our civilization, a historical statement of the noble expression of our humanity.

Conservatives see no need for public support for art. Believing instead that the Arts should be self supporting, often with the accompanying remark: *"I don't like it, I don't understand it and I don't want to pay for it".*

Many municipalities are now requiring developers to set aside a percentage of construction costs, usually about 1%, for public art.

A few artists are able to self-finance their artworks. One example of self financed artworks is that of the artists Christo and Jeanne-Claude who sold pieces of their own artwork, including preparatory drawings to finance their projects. Two of their most viewed installation artworks were *Running Fence*, (September 10-24, 1976), consisted of a veiled fence 24.5 miles long extending across the hills of Sonoma and Marin and ended in the Pacific Ocean. The 18 foot high fence was composed of 2,050 white nylon panels suspended by steel cables. The other: *The Gates (February 12, 2005 through February 27, 2005)* which consisted of 7,503 saffron-colored nylon panels stretching along 23 miles of pathways in Central Park, New York City.

One public Artwork financed completely by donations from individuals and corporations is *Cloud Gate* by British artist Anish Kapoor. Situated in Millennium Park, Chicago, Illinois, it is an elliptical shaped, seamless, stainless steel structure with a mirror-like surface that reflects the Chicago skyline. It measures 33 by 66 by 42 feet and weighs 100 tons. Its elliptical shape distorts and twists the reflected image.

Arguments favoring governmental support of the Arts cover several themes. Often sighted is that Art Education, exposing youngsters to art fosters imagination and facilitates the child's educational success. It is a way for disadvantaged children to experience education in a positive and creative manner.

Art creates jobs and produces tax revenues, especially from tourists. Public art creates a sense of place, history and speaks of the quality of the human endeavor. With two million full-time artists and nearly six million art-related jobs in this country, arts jobs are real jobs that are part of the real economy. Art workers pay taxes, and art contributes to economic growth, neighborhood revitalization, and the livability of American towns and cities. Public art invigorates public spaces; It can make us pay attention to our civic environment. It leaves a legacy for the future.

We humans do art because we are human. We are by nature creative. Art expression is a method of communication; we tell stories of our lives, our shared histories, or experiences both tragic and comical. Art chronicles our own lives and experiences over time. We need art to understand and share our history. Art practice requires us to think, to be reflective and to be inspired. It stimulates our brains. Without art we do not have culture. Past cultures had art. We know past civilizations by their culture, by their artistic accomplishments; not so much who their politicians, kings, popes or rules were, but by their artists. We know of Leonardo da Vinci, Michelangelo, Rembrandt, Claude Monet, Paul Cezanne and countless great artists from earlier times. Could you name the Pope, King or Emperor of their times? Art is the language that all people speak, across racial, cultural, social, educational, and economic barriers. Art enhances cultural appreciation and awareness. Art raises the ordinary to the extraordinary.

"You find art-making in every culture. It's a genetically predisposed activity, much like language. To say that its sole reason is to confer advantage in sexual selection is far too limiting."
CHARLES DARWIN'S DESCENT OF MAN

11

Four Horsemen of the Apocalypse Revised Book of Revelation

POPULATION GROWTH, CLIMATE Crisis, the Disparity of Wealth and *Homo sapiens* Intrinsic Nature; all four are all interlinked. Could these four 'Horsemen" be the causative agent in the presumptive "demise of civilization as we know it"? *Demise of Civilization As We Know It*; this classic phrase has been used extensively by writers. It adds a certain pizzazz to any heading. My interpretation: *The future is dire.*

Population Growth

We are well over 7 billion people; 7,142,976,392 as of this moment. Currently there is a net gain of about 3 persons per second. http://www.census.gov. Doing the math, 300,000 people per day, 94 million people per year. That's equivalent to eleven New York Cities each year. I see no sign of a downward trend. There is a finite amount of resources on earth. Any suggestions?

In 1958 my professor at UCSB, Dr. Wally Muller, lectured about population growth. Then, the world's population was about 2.8 billion and he thought that number of people was too great to sustain quality life. He noted that 10 years earlier, 1948, the population was 2.3 billion. He was alarmed that the world population had increased by 1/2 billion people in just 10 years, a 22% increase. We now have, in the intervening 68 years, increased the population nearly three times. I am certain he would be utterly shocked and dismayed of the present situation. Projections are that we will reach over 16 billion by century's end (if we don't all kill ourselves off).

In 1798, the world's population was about one billion people. That is the year Thomas Malthus, (1766-1834) wrote *An Essay on the Principle of Population.* Malthus was a British cleric and scholar in political economics and demography. His essay argued that population growth increases exponentially while the food supply increased arithmetically. The inevitable consequence is that people would outstrip available food. To forestall the dire consequences, he proposed preventive measures; either with moral restraints such as abstinence or delay of marriages or by restricting marriages of people suffering poverty or having 'defects'. Without curtailing population, war, epidemics and famine would surely occur.

What Malthus could not know is that 'modernization' of farming would postpone temporarily the intersect of population and starvation. One of the most significant processes that changed agriculture was the discovery that ammonia, the bases of fertilizers, could be synthesized from hydrogen and nitrogen. Fritz Haber, (1868-1934) a German chemist, received the Nobel Prize in Chemistry in 1918 for his tabletop demonstration of the catalytic formation of ammonia from hydrogen and nitrogen under conditions of high temperature and pressure. Together with Carl Bosch (1874-1940), Haber then developed an industrial process to produce fertilizers as well as explosives. Bosch also received his Nobel Laureate in Chemistry in 1931.

Prior to this time, there were two methods of increasing crop yields; natural fertilizers from animal wastes, dung; or alternatively farmers rotated crops with legumes, which fix nitrogen naturally.

Unintended Consequences. Ironically, these two, who invented the commercialized production of ammonia, increased the world's food supply and consequently the world's population by billions. They are also indirectly responsible for the destruction of millions of people, as ammonia is a constituent of explosives.

In 1968, when the earth's population had grown to about 3.5 billion, Paul Ehrlich published "The Population Bomb" contending that the battle to feed all of humanity was over. Paul Ehrlich, Professor of Biology at Stanford University, believed that nothing could be done. He warned of the mass starvation of humans that would occur in the 1970s and 1980s due to overpopulation, as well as other major societal upheavals, and advocated immediate action to limit population growth. Since the book's publication, the world's population has doubled.

The major factor to this more recent population growth is *The Green Revolution*. Norman Borlaug (1914 – 2009) was an American agronomist, humanitarian and Nobel Laureate and is recognized as the Father of the Green Revolution. He is credited with saving over one billion people from starvation. He was instrumental in the introduction of modern agricultural production techniques, hybridized seeds and synthetic fertilizers and pesticides to farmers of Mexico, Pakistan and India.

Feed and Breed; words that rhyme and are linked.

During my university school year, 1960-61, I took a year off my from my studies and with my two friends, Jurgen Hilmer and Pete Rezendes, we traveled through Europe and across North Africa, from Morocco to Egypt. We had an older VW van in which we slept, cooked and traveled; the classic 1960's adventure. In Egypt, we traveled from Alexandra to Cairo, to the Pyramids of Giza and on up the Nile towards Aswan. On the way up the Nile we were invited to visit a sugar cane refinery and to meet with the director of the refinery. During our visit we discussed the Aswan dam, still under construction, with aid from the USSR. He discussed the benefits that this dam would bring to Egypt. Damming the Nile would prevent the annual flooding. Also there could be year round water available to irrigate greater acreage; hence a greater abundance of food. Unemployment was high and damming the Nile River would certainly improve living conditions for the Egyptians.

My thought at the time, and we discussed this, is that with increased food production, would this not lead to increased population growth and hence the same standard of living? The Director acknowledged that the population would increase. In 1961 the population of Egypt was 28 million, essentially all living along a narrow strip of land boarding the Nile River. Today, the population exceeds 83 million. They are still impoverished and political turmoil has increased.

In addition, there were two unforeseen consequences of the Aswan Dam. The annual flood waters had brought nutrients down the Nile and into the Mediterranean sea. The flooding ceased as well as their shrimping industry. The nutrients were vital for the shrimp. The second consequence was that since there was year round irrigation of fields, there was a much higher incidence of schistosomiasis. Schistosomiasis is a parasitic disease caused by trematodes. These worms spend part of their life cycle in snails and the other half in mammals; in the Egyptian case, humans. With increased flooded fields, the population of snails increased and, of course, the incidence of this disease. Egyptian farmers are now wearing rubber boots and gloves when tending their fields. While the mortality rate of schistosomiasis is low, there is damage to internal organs, and in children, impaired growth and cognitive development.

The United Nations Food and Agriculture Organization estimates that nearly 870 million people of the 7.1 billion people in the world, or one in eight, were suffering from chronic undernourishment in 2010-2012. Almost all the hungry people, 852 million, live in developing countries, representing 15 percent of the population of developing counties. There are 16 million people undernourished in developed countries". http://www.worldhunger.org

So there! Once again, humans, when faced with an impending disaster, rise to the occasion to stave off the disaster - or more realistically, we just postponed what will be a greater disaster. Feed the world and you merely increase the number of impoverished humans. What comes to my mind: Humans are cunning. We're at 7 billion and counting.

Banning religion is very unrealistic. Folks cling to their religion and religious leaders need more followers--an inseparable combination.

The future is of no concern for the religious leaders; only salvation for those already here. The Catholic church's stand on women rights, abortion and birth control is archaic and not likely to change. The church is ruled by men and that won't change. Humans continue to reproduce at rates greater than replacement.

Spike the Coke. Create a great tasting soft drink, such as the popular Coca Cola but with the addition of a birth control drug; and distribute it free or at a very low cost. I wonder what religious groups, pro-growth advocates and paranoid nationalist would say to such a suggestion. Realistically, nothing can be done. Live with it and be prepared for the consequences. What more could be said?

The Climate Crisis

"We are all born ignorant, but one must work hard to remain stupid"
BENJAMIN FRANKLIN

It changed from Global Warming to Climate Change and now Climate Crisis. Regardless how one labels this manmade phenomenon, it's here and it's real. What are we to do? And the world"s population is exploding. We're stymied by politicians and theologians. What can we do to change the views of members of congress such as Darrel Issa and Daniel Inohof? Have they read the reports on climate change; shall we force them to read it? Send them back to college to take some basic science courses? Take away their Bibles? How can they ignore scientific evidence? Here's the answer: take away the money they receive from Fossil Fuel corporations and Super Pacs.

"Complex societies have sometimes survived the rise and fall of empires, plagues, wars and famines. They won't survive six degrees of climate change, sustained for a millennium. In return for 150 years of explosive consumption, much of which does nothing to advance human welfare, we are atomising the natural world and the human systems that depend on it."
GEORGE MONBLOT, THE GUARDIAN DECEMBER 3, 2012

Conservative groups may have spent up to $1billion a year on the effort to deny science and oppose action on climate change. The anti-climate effort has been largely underwritten by conservative billionaires, often working through secretive funding networks. They have displaced corporations as the prime supporters of 91 think tanks, advocacy groups and industry associations which have worked to block action on climate change. http://www.wired.co.uk/news/archive/2013-12/21/denial

Every report I have read on the subject of climate over the past 40 years has continually shorten the time of the arctic melt; a summer when the Northwest passage is ice free. The polar ice caps have melted faster in last 20 years than in the last 10,000. The latest study suggests that the Northwest Passage could be ice-free by the year 2016.

Ashutosh Jogalekar, March 6, 2013, Scientific American.

Climatologists, thousands of them, use multiple resources to take measurements of the earth. Satellites are used to measure ice and glacial flows, to map rain forest retreats and the rate of desertification. They can measure radiances in various wavelength bands and then calculate temperatures of the atmosphere, land and water and map the oscillations of oceanic waters. Ice core samples from glaciers and the polar caps can reveal ancient temperatures and atmospheric compositions.

Scientists trek out on to glaciers and the tundra and go on oceanic explorations; they all are measuring and observing the changes that are occurring as the temperature slowly increases. Climatologists examine ancient pollen samples, limestone deposits, they measure tree rings; they scour the earth looking for clues concerning the warming of the earth. They publish their observations and analysis in peer reviewed journals. A peer reviewed scientific report is one that has been evaluated by other academics, competent in that specialized field; experts that can evaluate the veracity of the research. From listening to the skeptics, one would think climatologists merely stick a moist finger in the air, check the direction of the wind and then huddle together to dream up their conclusions (conspiracy). Climatologists work very hard and are dedicated to obtaining results, not concocting conspiracies.

The really discomforting problem is that too few humans that take the time to read and understand the crisis. Greater participation by the public is necessary to change the politics that this crisis has generated. The enormous profits accumulated by the Petroleum Industry would not have been possible without the cozy relationship between money and politics.

Disparity of Wealth

"It is neither wealth nor splendor, but tranquility and occupation which give you happiness."
THOMAS JEFFERSON

Oxfam has recently reported that the World's 85 richest individuals have same wealth as 3.5 billion of the poorest. Translation: 0.0000012% of the earth's population controls 50% of the total wealth. The wealth of the 1% richest people in the world amounts to $110 trillion or 65 times as much as the poorest 50% of the world. Oxfam also argues that this is no accident either, saying growing inequality has been driven by a "power grab" by wealthy elites, who have co-opted the political process to rig the rules of the economic system in their favor.

http://www.theguardian.com/business/2014/jan/20/oxfam-85-richest-people-half-of-the-world

In November 2013, the World Economic Forum released its 'Outlook on the Global Agenda 2014', in which it ranked widening income disparities as the second greatest worldwide risk in the coming 12 to 18 months. Based on those surveyed, inequality is 'impacting social stability within countries and threatening security on a global scale.'

World Economic Forum (2013) 'Outlook on the Global Agenda 2014', Geneva: World Economic Forum, http://www3.weforum.org/docs/WEF_GAC_GlobalAgendaOutlook_2014.pdf

In September, 2013, a UC Berkeley study found that between 2009 to 2012, the average real income per family in the U.S. for the top 1% grew by 31.4%. The bottom 99% incomes grew by only 0.4%. Hence, the top 1% captured 95%

of the income gains for these three years. http://elsa.berkeley.edu/~saez/saez-UStopincomes-2012.pdf

When one percent of Americans own 40 percent of the U.S. wealth and with 442 billionaires in the U.S., can there be a true democracy?

The *Citizens United v. Federal Commissions*, a constitutional law case in which the U.S. Supreme Court held that the First Amendment prohibits the government from restricting political independent expenditures by corporations, associations or labor unions. In the majority opinion: *"The appearance of influence or access, furthermore, will not cause the electorate to lose faith in our democracy."*

Corporations and billionaires spend billions of dollars each year on campaigns and lobbying advocacy. In 2009, the health care industry spent more than $263 million on lobbyists. Do you think the lobbyist receive good value? Have you noticed the big drop in drug prices and medical costs? Have you noticed the fancy cars and homes owned by the executives of the health care and insurance industries? Hard to notice; they are all within gated communities.

> *"Last week, the Supreme Court reversed a century of law to open the floodgates for special interests — including foreign corporations — to spend without limit in our elections. Well I don't think American elections should be bankrolled by America's most powerful interests, or worse, by foreign entities."*
> PRESIDENT OBAMA, 2010 STATE OF THE UNION ADDRESS

A 2008 study by Princeton professors Larry M. Bartels and Christopher Achen, found that *"voters often misperceive what life has been like during the incumbent's administration. They are inordinately focused on the here and now, mostly ignoring how things have gone earlier in the incumbent's term. And they have great difficulty judging which aspects of their own and the country's well-being are the responsibility of elected leaders and which are not."* Larry M. Bartels. How Smart is the American Voter?, Los Angeles Times, November 3, 2008

Combine the wealth of a few individuals together with their corporations financing those political TV ads in support of the (re)election of "their" Members of Congress: what is the result? More of the same.

Higher education is not highly valued by conservative's standards. They would deny this. They say they value teachers but they support public funding of private schools, "Charter Schools", where religious agenda can be taught without the governmental interference. Bonds for funding of public schools fail repeatedly often the result of conservatives messages. After all, an unenlightened electorate is easier to bamboozle.

One of the factors contributing to the disparity of wealth is the cost of higher education. The middle and lower economic classes are at a severe financial handicap paying tuition at a university. I've read estimates of one hundred thousands dollars as the present cost of a college education. At prestigious universities, the cost can be closer to $170,000. Jobs are disappearing, either going overseas or replaced by robotic machines. The economy is recovering, but the joblessness remains. Corporations have no interest in this human dilemma; they cannot have empathy; they are not people. On second thought, just what was the ruling of the Supreme Court's The *Citizens United v. Federal Commissions* law case?

The jobs of the future are either in the service industry or jobs that require a high level of training and education. The service jobs are at wages insufficient to support a family. Family assistance programs are being cut (to bring down the national debt). High paying jobs, those requiring a college or university education, require substantial costs, mostly unavailable excepting for those children coming from rich families or those willing to take on substantial debt. Bank of America is doing quite well issuing student loans. Students with these loans will be working for the banks for decades. In the late 1950's when I attended university, I was able to finance my education by part time and summer jobs without taking on any debt or student loans. I received no financial assistance. California's wise leaders, *pre*-Ronald Reagan, realized the need for educated people for California's future. Tuition fees were nonexistent *then* for residents. Total University fees were under 100 dollars per semester. Anyone with the desire and qualifications could attend the university. I managed just fine; not a feasible plan today.

Homo sapiens' Intrinsic Nature

Are *Homo sapiens* a Noble Savage? Are we incorruptible as we have innate goodness? Is our moral compass genetically determined? The questions we should ask of ourselves: are the original The Four Horsemen of the Apocalypse,

Conquest, War, Famine and Death a foretelling of our future? Or are we just savages.

The term *noble savage* is a literary stereotype that characterizes the impoverished outsider as not to have been corrupted by civilization and hence symbolizes humanity's innate goodness. The term has been used since the 17th century in various fashions. The 3rd Earl of Shaftesbury in his Inquiry Concerning Virtue (1699) postulated that the moral sense in humans is natural and innate and based on feelings rather than resulting from the indoctrination of a particular religion. Charles Dickens used the word in an oxymoronic sense in his 1851 sarcastic review of the London exhibition of the work of George Catlins' painting of American Indians. In his essay, entitled The Noble Savage, Dickens expressed repugnance for Indians and their way of life in scathingly terms, recommending that they ought to be "civilized out of existence".

We humans may be warriors. We may inflict pain needlessly. We may be excessively selfish. Are the congressional Militaristic Interventionists genetically predisposed to wage war? Are these individuals capable of rational analysis of the situation or are they just posturing? Is their hawkishness similar to a peacock display; an eagerness to copulate or an eagerness to invade? I don't have the answer; just a thought.

"Life is like a game of cards. The hand you are dealt is determinism: the way you play it is free will."
JAWAHARIAL NEHRU

The issue of Free Will has been debated throughout history including not only whether free will exists but even how to define the concept. The opposing view of Free Will would be determinism. Hardline determinists would argue that human behavior is not only predictable but ordained by our genetic constitution.

We all seem to know what Free Will is and we all believe we have it. We have the choice to go to the beach, or not, but once there, can we not notice the babe in the bikini, especially if she is large breasted? I can go or stay home; dependent upon the weather or other factors; your choice, well contemplated.

A beautiful woman sauntering in front of us; would you not check her out? Do you really have a choice? Did the old hormones take over? When I called my friend a Jew, was this an example of Free Will or was I acting out of instinct? Now I expect you to say: "But wait a minute, I have Free Will. I can choose which stocks to buy based upon my market research. I can make an analytical decision". Can you switch religions, or political parties? Consider the power of religion. Huge churches preaching that you will go to hell, if you doubt their word. No heaven for you. Our political beliefs are similarly intrenched.

One definition: Free Will is the ability to make choices without constraints, without the influences of theological, physical, social or mental constraints; the ability to act at one's own discretion. Is it possible for *Homo sapiens to* act at one's own discretion when the decisions that one makes takes place in our brain? Many of mankind's behaviors are constrained or influenced by deeply held religious or political beliefs. So exactly what is free will and do we have it? Does Madison Avenue know how to influence your buying habits? Has Madison Avenue insidiously placed a computer virus-like behavioral module into you; have you been hacked? Here is a thought problem: does a wolf in the wild have free will?

"Divine intervention? If you were god and your creation created such a mess, would you intervene?"
Oliver Sacks

All life here on earth is hydrocarbon based; an ensemble of water, proteins, carbohydrates, fats and nucleic acids. We are animals with an intellect. *Homo sapiens* are the product of a long evolutionary process. We having a brain, a neurological network that is encoded by our genetics, our DNA, which has ancestrally roots.

Our senses receive input from the outside and together with our memory and the wiring within we reach decisions and take actions. Are we freely making decisions or are they 'flavored' by fear or by dogmatic teachings?

That's about all there is to us. One species arose to such dominance as to have the ability to destroy itself. Was this God's plan? Did he get it wrong? Did man not stick to the plan? What could happen if God started over? God would need to start with the same building blocks, the ones found on the Periodic Table. Would these "new" life forms be tolerant and rational and not participate in slavery, wars or mass shootings?

Would his second attempt be any more successful? Maybe this is already his fourth or fifth attempt. Or is this exactly what he planned; competition and survival of the fittest? Maybe Donald Trump is God's emblematic human specimen, a triumph; just as God planned. Donald Trump is rich, famous, very good looking, sponsor of beauty pageants, a self proclaimed environmentalist and builder of a golf course and resort adjacent to an environmentally sensitive coastal dune system in Scotland. Word is that he's building a University in Scotland to study Biodiversity as well as building an AID's clinic in Kenya to honor President Obama.

12

The Middle -or The End

"Man masters nature not by force but by understanding. This is why science has succeeded where magic failed: because it has looked for no spell to cast over nature."
JACOB BRONOWSKI

FROM *AUSTRALOPITHECUS SEDIBA to Homo ergaster* to *Homo heidelbergensis to Homo sapiens*; a most fascinating journey. Here we are, you and I are along with 7 billion other humans on this great blue marble.

Why can't we all: "Live Together in Perfect Harmony"
EBONY AND IVORY (1982) PAUL MCCARTNEY AND STEVIE WONDER

WE COMMENCED THIS critique of *Homo sapiens'* traits and behaviors by presenting some history of our ancestors. Paleoanthropologists have dug up some interesting relatives of ours. They are still digging; there will certainly be more of our cousins to be discovered. Throughout, I have purposefully used both words, *human* and *Homo sapiens*. I wanted to make clear that humans are presently in a sticky mess and this mess can be attributed to the fact that we belong to the species of animals called *Homo sapiens*. All too often we make decisions irrationally, without deep contemplation and considerations. Humans can display, at times, some unsavory human traits: anger, hate, loathing, stubbornness, and prejudices. These traits are fueled by our delusions, false memories and the lack of a liberal education. These often lead to unwarranted fears, which, at times, guides us in making public policies. Some of these policies are non-beneficial to human's survival. We value wealth as the measure of success. Empathy and cooperation are not as well valued. We are *Homo sapiens*. Are *Homo sapiens* a Noble Savage? Are we incorruptible as we have innate goodness? Is our moral compass genetically determined? The questions we should ask of ourselves: are the original *The Four Horsemen of the Apocalypse, Conquest, War, Famine and Death* a foretelling of our future? Or are we just Savages?

All life on earth is special; however humans believe that we are extra special. In the broadest sense, *Homo sapiens* are just one of the many. We human beings can attain the status of a nobel species and insure a bright future for generations to come. The brain we are born with is not a blank slate. The brain comes already programmed with software, software that has originated in our ancient ancestors. Traits have been selected that have insured our survival. I presented my perspective of *Homo sapiens* and our traits. I have proposed that there are good traits and there are bad traits. Simply, good traits lead to the continuance of our species in relative comfort. Bad traits are those that may lead to our demise. These traits may be hardwired, but our brain is programable. Our brains have a huge capacity to learn.

Do humans recognize that there is really a problem? This might be the problem; not comprehending that there is a problem. Most all scientifically educated individuals, those who understand the climate crisis, would say that there is an impending crisis. The only uncertainty is the severity and the arrival date. The public's lack of interest or understanding is alarming. Most people are not engaged or interested in worldly affairs. Unless the crisis is immediate and local, there is little concern. If a bridge fails, it is a crisis only if it disrupts our journey. If the bridge is on the opposite side of the country; the event won't register in our consciousness. Lack of compassion and empathy for those affected are all too common. Greed, selfishness and complacency; *Homo sapiens* traits. Surely Moms don't teach their youngsters those bad behavior.

My observation is that the majority of youth seems not concerned about future events. There are at least two factors which contribute to this. Teenagers' brains are still developing; judgment is not mature. Furthermore, youth are rebellious, by nature. Keeping abreast of world events is what adults do, not what teenagers do. Video games, texting friends and keeping abreast of the latest in popular music occupies the interest of many youth. That's their nature. Too much on their plate, too many friends that need updating. This is not a commendation; just an observation. It is what it is. My conclusion: it's a shame, it's their world that is in peril.

I am not completely disillusioned by young people. The unexpected sometimes occur. When, during my years as a student at John Marshall Junior High School in Pasadena, there were annual Student Body Presidency elections. The candidates were offered a forum where each candidate spoke presenting their ideas for a more perfect student body. I remember the two individuals running for class President; Cathy, a bright normal looking teenage girl along with a popular football player. I don't recall the football player's name, but I do remember Cathy. Her pledge was to increase student support for all the usual reasons and so forth. I do not remember exactly any of her pledges, excepting they all seemed reasonable and admirable. The footballer pledged to replace the water in the schools water fountains with Coca Cola. Everyone thought that this was a great idea; free Coke. Not many initially considered the feasibility. What a brilliant idea to garnish all the kids votes. Time to vote; it wasn't that close. Cathy won. Rationality prevailed, even for young people. The unexpected occurs, sometimes.

The future will be in the hands of the youth. It is to be hoped that there will be sufficient numbers of young people that will be educated and motivated to take up the challenge. There are scholastic activities that attract the youth: Science Fairs, Spelling Bees and other academic challenges that afford the young to be champions. Unfortunately, high school football games are better attended.

The expression; "Man's Inhumanity to Man and to the Planet" may seem trite or just a cliché. Either sentiment is easily dismissing the acuteness of the Human Condition.

Our present environment is vastly different from what early man faced. We are now faced with quite different challenges; Over-Population, the Climate

Crisis and poorly educated congressional leadership together with a populace equally undereducated. We have divided ourselves into two classes; the super rich and ruling class who control political decisions, and the rest of us who just seem to follow.

We can strive towards loftiness. We need to be better educated in the sciences and the humanities. We should strive to be humane. Place rationality higher; be more like Mr. Spock, but with compassion, understanding and charity in our behaviors. Long term goals, our survival should take priority. We may be "locked" into behavioral patterns that we inherited genetically from our ancient ancestors, but the nurture we acquire can aspire us to be better. We have the capacity to "all get along". We do have choices and the choices we make will determine humans' survivability.

One could look at life on earth as a game, which is terminated when humanity no longer exists on this planet. Perhaps life is just *One Grand Uncontrolled Journey, A Marvelous Spectacle* or *God's Experiment.* We have the privilege of not only witnessing it; we are the actors, the principals-front and center. My grand question is: how long will humanity survive in relative comfort; thousand of years, hundreds? My best guess is that time is limited, maybe just a few dozen years. We have warlike traits and if our own resources become limited, we will just look to our neighbors to replenish. Other organisms will continue to exist for millions of years, but humans have, in my estimation, a much more limited time, especially if you postulate that a certain quality of life is important. I really don't believe that humans can continue on as we have in the past. Our path is littered with the detritus of our life style. Something must change or we shall end up as two tribes on an island called --*Lord of the Flies.*

> *How will it all end; life on earth? Astrobiologist Jack O'Malley-James has written that "all animals and plants will vanish from the Earth within the next billion years. The sun will get hotter, causing greater evaporation, which will reduce carbon dioxide levels. This will mean there is eventually too little CO2 for plants to survive. When they die out, herbivores will also die out, followed by carnivores. Microbes will then be all that remains until another billion years later when the seas will also dry out. Very little life will remain."*
>
> Daily Mail, 1 July 2013.

A billion years is of no concern for me and likely no concern even for our great grandchildren. What's the fuss? We have plenty of time, time to the final collapse, however an undesirable environment may soon become evident. What is stopping us?

Changing Belief Systems

Murphy's Law states that if something can go wrong, it will. One variation: laboratory animals, when tested under ideally controlled conditions, will do as they damn well please. Seems applicable to humans. We do as we please. Given that fear, anger, irrational behavior and loathing are hardwired, can humans change? When confronting an individual with a opposite point of view, change is difficult. Point out the fact that the earth is warming and that humans put 100 million tons of carbon dioxide is put into the atmosphere daily, denial is often the response of half of the population. Common responses are; the earth isn't warming or warming is a natural cycle or the trees will take up the carbon dioxide. Denial is a human trait. How can we change someone's beliefs? I think most people may believe that it is possible, but only with great difficulty.

Homo sapiens are but one of millions of species on earth. We have characteristics; behaviors and traits that arose millions of years ago and were stuck with them. We think and decide using the soft grey matter called the brain; the same sort of brain all primates have. There's no possibility that natural, or artificial selection can eliminate undesirable traits. It might be nice to "clone" out our warlike nature and live in perfect harmony. That won't happen. Humans may want to change the belief of, say a friend, to believe in their religion or that climate change is real and that it's manmade. We don't have thousands of years to make the change in another's beliefs. Selective breeding is not a choice.

There are a few major changes to our "belief system" that have occurred rather rapidly. For instance, our stance about Iraq. George W. Bush went on TV to tell Americans about the *Axis of Evil* and that one of the evil ones was Saddam Hussein who had weapons of Mass Destruction. He even introduced us to the acronym WMD, then not common in most people's vocabulary. We were told that destruction of the USA and our allies was imminent. That language scared the bejesus out of us; even some of the liberals were scared. Fear was in the air. It worked, we invaded; "Operation Iraqi Freedom". It took about a little over a year for President Bush and his neoconservatives to change a whole nation's beliefs. Wrong country, but who in the Bush administration wasn't ready to kick some butt, any butt?

> *"Call me a converted skeptic. Three years ago I identified problems in previous climate studies that, in my mind, threw doubt on the very existence of global warming. Last year, following an intensive research effort involving a dozen scientists, I concluded that global warming was real and that the prior estimates of the rate of warming were correct. I'm now going a step further: Humans are almost entirely the cause".*
> RICHARD A. MULLER, A PROFESSOR OF PHYSICS AT THE UNIVERSITY OF CALIFORNIA, BERKELEY, NYTIMES, JULY 28, 2012.

Professor Muller stated that it required extensive review of the scientific literature and discussion with experts to change his perspective. He initially thought that the evidence did not warrant the conclusion that climate change was real and manmade. However, with rationality and close examination of the data, he changed.

Many individuals are immune to rational thought when certain subjects are brought up; politics, religion and even personal relationships. Anger is a common response. There never seems to be sufficient information to shake their beliefs. A friendly discussion turns argumentative with denial of the evidence, countered with arguments that support their position. Often they do not listen. Civil discussions are useless. Why is the brain so resistant to change? Is there a fear 'module"?

There seems to be no simple and practical solution available to change the belief system of some people. Few have the intellect and rationality of Professor Richard Muller. How would you convince a coal miner in West Virginia to embrace climate change? His livelihood depends upon coal.

Howard Gardner, of the Harvard Business School has offered ideas, mostly applicable for the business world: *"Present promising idea with enough frequency and variety that others will understand it, remember it, and, most important, embrace it".* Changing Minds: The Art and Science of Changing Our Own and Other People's Minds *(Harvard Business School Press, 2004),*

As a summary Dr. Gardner suggests the following. Say it often and in many ways in a variety of formats. Frame your message objectively in neutral and familiar terms. Provide contrasting scenarios; a devil advocate's perspective. Importantly, know your audience's intelligence. Select the right blend of descriptions and representations.

Susan K. Perry, Ph.D., a social psychologist suggest 5 Ways to Change Someone's Mind: Keep the message simple. Perceived self-interest; it's in their best interest. Incongruity; some surprising feature or attribute. Show confidence in your point of view. Display empathy. Psychology Today, May 15, 2011.

There you have it. Sounds easy.

"I do my best work when I am in pain and turmoil".
STING

"The best thinking has been done in solitude. The worst has been done in turmoil".
THOMAS EDISON

Conflicting strategies. From my perspective, we can expect turmoil. We have become divided into tribes. We are divided by skin color, religion, language, politics and we end up with many groups shouting at each other. An attempt to build bridges between countries is the United Nations. It has certainly been effective in many instances, but there are a few who fear that we Americans will be ruled by some despot from some other foreign evil state. By the numbers, Conservatives and Liberals are, in most countries, nearly equally divided. Our tribes argue continuously. Each side has compelling arguments. Their views are often mutually exclusive. It is the level or degree of fear that we assign to situations which all too often guide us. We are conservatives because we are self-centric, fearing that we will run out of money and that the other side will cause havoc. We are liberal because we have compassion for the less fortunate; we want to be one big happy family. We fear the consequences if the other side has the power. Our brains "assign" our level of fear assessment based upon our genetics and our experiences; a balance of nurture and nature.

When you realize that the neurological pathways, the flow of neurotransmitters and signals swirling around in your brain, dictate your decision when facing a threatening situation, you have a chance to minimize the consequences by taking considered action. Obviously if a car is fast approaching in your path, jump out of the way. If a politician tells you death and starvation awaits you. Give pause. Fear can be crippling. Recall that your brain's first response to a threatening situation is the sending neurological signals directly to the amygdala without cognitive processing.

When my daughter was growing into a young woman, I had an opportunity to teach her how to deal with certain fears. We were walking in a rather seedy section of San Francisco after dark. A young man was approaching us. He appeared a bit suspect. Before he was too close to us, I told her to not look down at the pavement, don't exhibit fear, but instead look him over top to bottom and take a mental note of his physical appearance including his shoes, and clothing. Just look him over in an investigative fashion. Don't smile, don't look aggressive, but do acknowledge him with a slight nod. I don't know if he had any ulterior agendum other that to get to his destination, but the fact that we could have identified him may have prevented an unwelcome event. He just keep on his way. One's fear telegraphs a signal. You have something of value. Politicians send messages of fear. They want your vote.

"Darkness cannot drive out darkness: only light can do that.
Hate cannot drive our hate: only love can do that."
Martin Luther King, Jr.

Anger is the first step towards hate and revenge. Revenge can lead to some unpleasant consequences. Anger may start with a rather insignificant event. Let's say, during rush hour, a car takes cuts and snakes in line in front of you as you wait with others in a line of cars approaching an exit. Your immediate primitive response might be to flip him off or beep your car's horn. There might be reasonable excuses for his behavior. The driver might just had realized that this was his exit and he's late for an important meeting. The driver may not have realized that the long line of cars was for this exit. Maybe he's is just immature, lack empathy and feels a need to express his masculinity. There may be many possible reasons. The point is that you will be tardy to your destination by perhaps 4 or 5 seconds with him cutting in. Reacting negatively will only give him justification for his action; you're a jerk. Smiling and giving him a pleasant wave just might be a more positive response.

The lesson; carefully look at any fearful event, take note of all the characteristics, evaluate the severity of any possible negative event. Then act accordingly. Don't rush to judgment and think and believe the worse. This advise is relevant to those TV political ads and murmurings from politicians. Analyze their words and consider what their agenda might be. If they promise to put free coke in every drinking fountain....

If I were to be anointed God, with humans being what they are, my first action would be to speak to all humans and say: *"You're on your own. I can't help you. Don't waste your time honoring me or hoping that I will give you directions"*. I would be emphatic. *"No help for you. Don't invoke some mumbo jumbo from a book I didn't write. Don't use that manmade ancient book to justify your bad behavior. If you want to be humane, then quick killing others in my name. Have more sex and if you do, then be sure to use contraceptives, for God's sake. Be more like the Bonobos."*

Bonobos, *Pan paniscus,* is a great ape and one of two species in the genus *Pan*, the other is *Pan troglodytes*, or common chimpanzee. The bonobo is known for its high level of sexual behavior. Sex functions in conflict appeasement, affection, social status, excitement, and stress reduction. It occurs in virtually all partner combinations and in a variety of positions. This is a factor in the lower levels of aggression seen in the bonobo when compared to the common chimpanzee and other apes. Bonobos are perceived to be matriarchal and a male's rank in the social hierarchy is often determined by his mother's rank.

Have we found the answer to human's aggressive behavior? Should we live our lives as the bonobos; frequent and unencumbered sexual encounters? Should females have a higher ranking than males? Bonobos have survived for ten million years. Of course, their cultural development is substantially less than *Homo sapiens*, no flat screen TVs and the rest of niceties of modern society. Bonobos are more advanced in one category: no wars.

There is another alternative. Forget compassion, join the Tea Party. Deny the Climate Crisis. Invest in Exxon-Mobil, Halliburton and Monsanto. Practice Laissez-faire. Get government out of the way of Capitalism, except for instituting restrictive moral codes. Be in it for yourself. Read the Bible. Pray. God will save you. Simply outwit, out play and outlast.

Perhaps we should listen to Joel Osteen. He delivers a message of Hope; God will provide. On second thought, forget Joel. Instead be like Mahatma Gandhi. Live simple, don't covet designer outfits, don't wage war, and don't torture others either for their secrets or for a thrill. Be a pacifist. Practice nonviolent civil disobedience, protest against wealth disparity, discrimination, poverty, man's wrongs but do support women's and minorities' rights.

Occam's razor states entities should not be multiplied unnecessarily. This principle is attributed to the 14th century English logician and Franciscan friar, William of Ockham (c. 1287 - 1347). The principle has been stated as: The simplest explanation with the fewest assumptions is more likely to be accurate than more complicated explanations.

Humans put 100 million tons of carbon dioxide into the atmosphere each day. Carbon dioxide is a green house gas. The earth's temperature is increasing. The polar ice caps are melting. Your thoughts? Will each of us leave a legacy that will make us proud of having been a member of the species *Homo sapiens* on this great blue marble? "*Take only photographs, leave only footprints*" is a motto of The Sierra Club.

Every time we perturb the environment, its changes and there will be consequences. We need a governor, a sensibility system to regulate and to ensure a steady state. Capitalism is unsustainable. Even socialism need a governor. Humans have the ability to regulate their core body temperature. If you are too hot, you sweat releasing heat. If you're too cold, you shiver, moving muscles involuntarily to generate heat. You can't stay off your set temperature too long. Economic growth cannot be sustained, unless populations continue to increase and resources are unlimited.

"Hope in reality is the worst of all evils because it prolongs the torments of man."
FRIEDRICH NIETZSCHE

"Hope is a waking dream"
ARISTOTLE

Let's just hope for a better outcome. Emulate Billy Ray Cyrus. I think one could consider that hope is just a placebo; a harmless medicine that has no therapeutic effect, but may have a psychological benefit. Honestly, there may not be much we can do. Religion won't go away. Divisiveness between political parties will remain, or become even more divisive. Humans will continue to copulate with the consequence of more babies. All hope is lost. I would suggest that aspire is what we should do.

Most humans are honest and ethical, most want to be productive, most are creative and most have concerns for the rest of humanity. We contribute to 'save the rainforest' campaigns. We support charities that care for the hungry in America and Africa. We are appalled at the starving and orphaned children in the Sudan. Consider supporting or endowing charities whose goals are "Saving the Earth". There are many including The Natural Resources Defense Council (NRDC), Audubon Society, Nature Conservancy, Sierra Club and Planned Parenthood. There are many other worthwhile environmental causes and organizations. These organizations work to preserve our earth and our inhabitants. What a wonderful legacy that could be, with your support.

Remember Cathy, John Marshall Junior High School's class President. She offered reasoned agenda and the teenagers responded.

"Breathe. Let go. And remind yourself that this very moment is the only one you know you have for sure."
Oprah Winfrey

Don't Give Up - Come Out

Be a vegetarian. Switch to quinoa as a source of protein. Most animals produce carbon dioxide. The quinoa plant can use this gas to produce oxygen and protein. It takes at least 10 pounds of vegetation to produce one pound of beef; a partial solution to the climate crisis. Additionally, the cattle to table scenario uses more water than stopping at the vegetation stage. Problem solved.

On second thought, if the world were to switched to an all vegetarian diet, would that not only exacerbate the situation. Short term; more food for the starving. Long term, those previously starving people will have enough energy to procreate. And procreate they will. Remember my conversations at the sugar cane refinery in Egypt?

"Come out" of the bubble. If change is to happen, a critical mass needs to be generated. Politicians listen to polls. Politicians seem not to do what is right but what is expedient for their re-election. Simply stated, you can sit around and wait to see what happens or you can take action. If you believe that the sustainability of life, as we know it and want it to be is questionable, join a tribe.

There is a tribe whose members are composed of educated and reasoned individuals. Their core values are:

Religion should not dictate governmental or school policies.

The disparity between the super rich and the rest of the populace should be lessened; this disparity is destroying democracy.

Offshore bank accounts of US corporations and individuals should be taxed.

Access to the polls should not be infringed.

Better regulatory oversight of our natural resources.

Better regulation of corporate and private money over-influencing elections.

The Sciences and the Humanities should have greater governmental support.

Higher education and health care should be affordable for all.

Creation of jobs to develop a green economy and to repair our intra-structure.

Compassion

The Tribe's name: "The Liberals".

Liberals need to come out. Read and learn about the critical issues. Talk to your circle of friends about these critical issues. Aspire to be better informed. Remember the section on persuasion? The tips offered could be helpful in persuading others. Support financially environmental organizations and political candidates that promote your core values. Signing petitions, phone banking for your candidate, putting a bumper sticker on you car, standing on street corners with a banner or placard are easy and comforting, but generally do not affect change.

The Gays came out. First the daring; hair dressers, intellectuals and theater types. These avant-garde individuals were followed by other celebrities, athletes and ordinary people. Ellen DeGeneres came out, and she survived quite well. Anderson Cooper reported on gay issues quite extensively before he finally publicly admitted his gayness. Took him awhile, but he did come out. He too survived. Very few are now being dragged by rope behind a pickup truck bearing a Texas license plate. The result of the Come-Out is making headlines and most all are positive. If you were to 'come out' and become more active on the critical issues facing humanity, that just might be your legacy.

So the best advice is to live one's life fully, cause no harm and do well to others. To do harm, you may pay a price; pummeled, shunned or jailed. To do well towards others may reward you with fame, money, accolades or maybe nothing of note. Your kindness may go unnoticed. Making others have better lives has its rewards often immediately or later, or perhaps not at all. Self-satisfaction will be your reward. The realization that future generation of humans may continue is the reward.

Be Patriotic, not only for this country, but for earth. Patriotism should be more than just wearing a flag lapel pin or a "Support our Troops" bumper sticker. Remember the foofaraw Republicans made when early on, Obama didn't wear the flag lapel pin? What a fuss. Now, he's never seen without that symbol. Just what happens when one does, or does not wear that lapel pin? Is it really anymore relevant than a Green Bay Packer fan's wedged shape cheese hat. That team's fortunes probably don't rise or fall based on the number cheese hat wearing attendees. If I lived in Green Bay and was fortunate enough to have Packer season tickets, I'd probably wear one too. Camaraderie, Tailgate parties. I'm in! Sub-freezing temperatures; never mind.

'My fellow Americans, ask not what your country can do for you, ask what you can do for your country."
JOHN F. KENNEDY'S INAUGURAL ADDRESS, JANUARY 20, 1961

What happened to this sensibility? Patriots should be willing to help others less fortunate. Are Wall Street financiers and laissez-faire supporters considering others or only their individual financial well being? Are only conservatives patriots? Those individuals who weaken environmental laws, weaken banking laws, restrict voting rights, those who put religious values ahead of science in the class rooms; are they really patriotic? Exactly, who is a patriot? What sort of patriot are you? Do you support social justice and environmental causes for future generations? Have you given a hand up? Did you pay it forward?

Here is an idea: propose before congress legislation that limits congressional members to two terms only. Additionally, after leaving office they would be prohibited from joining either a Wall Street firm, a lobbying firm or a political advocacy group. Additionally, each departing member must become a public school teacher for a minimum of two years. They should know what teachers are paid and what teachers contribute to our nation. One additional caveat to this proposed law: their incoming and outgoing tax forms will be made public. Do you think this proposed legislation has a chance of becoming law?

One of Barack Obama's objectives as President is to have greater bi-partisanship in Congress. A nobel agendum, however success is in doubt. He does share the same concerns that I have; true equality for everyone, the role of the military in society, the disparity of wealth, the climate crisis, education, voting restrictions and universal health care. The opposition to the Affordable Care Act and many other of his agenda may, in part, be due to his "race". Prejudice still remains amongst many humans. He is pragmatic, realizing just what agenda can be accomplished during his presidency and what programs will require greater time. I would label President Obama as a pragmatic humanist.

"Try to learn something about everything and everything about something."
THOMAS HUXLEY

"Live as if you were to die tomorrow. Learn as if you were to live forever."
MAHATMA GANDHI

Become more learned. Read. When you don't know something, look it up. I highly recommend *Wikipedia*, a free Encyclopedia. I also suggest that you send them a few dollars. Wikipedia is a nonprofit corporation and depends upon the public for support. One of my most memorable professors was my Biochemistry Professor, Henry Nakada. Very occasionally when a fellow student asked a question, the answer to which he didn't know or remember, he would scratch his head, ponder and then say, *"Damn if I know"*. The next session he would have the answer. He was self-assured enough to admit he didn't know or remember everything and wise enough do some research to find the answer. For this honesty and wisdom, he is fondly remembered.

Be rational, be skeptical. Don't be rash. Consider the source of what you read and their agenda. Beware of the use of fear, as political operatives know the value of fear to direct behavior. When reading articles found in the magazines prominently displayed on supermarket newsstands, consider that most of these authors are not staff writers, but often freelance, eager for a pay check. Their writings may not be well researched.

Information that comes from respected scientific journals which are peer reviewed are more reliable. Most scientists are motivated by veracity as opposed to monetary considerations. Unfortunately, most scientific published papers are too advanced for most to understand. Fortunately, major newspapers have science writers who are able to present the information in a manner comprehendible to the lay public.

Go back to school. The community colleges are a wonderful source for your continued education. If you have not the inclination to go back to college, perhaps you should consider financially supporting or endowing your alma mater. In recent years, I have taken a series of Life Drawing classes. Yes, nude models, but that wasn't the reason. To draw well you must observe carefully not only the shape of the model, but the negative shape. Close observation is most important in art and in life. When I travel I take a sketch pad to draw what catches my attention. Drawing forces one to look carefully. You see more, you remember more. Your travel experiences are then so much more richer. I've also taken Art History classes at the community college. The history of human artistic accomplishment is wonderful. Another perk of taking adult classes is that the grade you receive could be absolutely inconsequential. Unless you are taking these classes for a degree, whether you pass with a grade of A or if you fail, your life goes on. You won't lose your job. When on your travels, you'll have a richer experience as you (and I hope you do) visit art museums. In my travel plans, art museums are a priority.

Take photographs. Memories-yes, but having a theme to your photography adds dimension and interest. Set up various albums. I have two themes. One is photographing bicycles and riders. I still bicycle, I still have my 1980's *Eddy Merckx* -full campy. It's now a classic; it's still a joy to ride. My other album is food; food brought to the table at the restaurants we visit. Other albums could be of street performers, bridges, boats, shop front windows, or street side vendors displaying a variety of colorful foods; most anything can bring great joy and remembrances. Recall the Easter Islanders; they did not have photography.

Be creative. Write a book. Wear kooky clothes occasionally to show your creative side. Go to museums, the symphony; applaud the youth showing their creativity. Ride a bicycle, hike nature trails, explore the wonders of nature. Visit our national parks. Buy a sketch pad and record your views of the world. Look for beauty. It can be found most anywhere, just be prepared for the unexpected. Take a careful look at a Picasso painting. Picasso took from nature and presented a representation as he saw it. The emergence of the image from his imagination would appear upon the canvas.

Be as imaginative as Picasso. Escape from the bubble; that constraint within which most people reside. Open your vistas. With our positive actions now, life on earth will be a bit less messy. The reasoned people that comprehend "The Issues" need to act. Don't follow the crowd just because. Be skeptical of outlandish claims. Are corporate interests your interests? Money should not be the only goal. Take a rational look at claims of political agenda. Open yourself to new ideas.

"What the World Needs Now Is Love"
HAL DAVID AND BURT BACHARACH. 1965

What the world needs now is love and compassion for the earth and for humanity. Hope and bumper stickers, are lovely but these don't address the problem; they won't lead to change. Spiking the Coke would be squashed and condemned as unethical, immoral and impractical.

The world needs individuals that have love, empathy and forward vision, towards all life on this planet, plant life and animal life. Each of us are just one of Trillions of other residents. Collectively *Homo sapiens* have not been the greatest of stewards but individually we should honor all life. We are one species of many other organisms that commenced living on a pristine earth. We have been fortunate to have been inhabitants at an amazing time. Amazing, not in the casual sense that is of common usage among teenagers. Amazing in the sense that in three billion years, life forms have evolved to where one species, *Homo sapiens*, are able to comprehend what life is; an elegance experience, complex, beautiful and fragile. Individually, we inhabit this earth for a relative short time. We should be accountable, at least to those yet to be born. Practice conservation, not conservative politics. Selfishness will not lead to survivability. Empathy, a very human trait, leads to compassion. We must have forward vision. Be creative. We need humane humans. What the world needs now are humans that practice random kindness and senseless acts of beauty. Inspire others, challenge yourself, vote and above all, behave smartly.

From Carl Sagan, Pale Blue Dot: A Vision of the Human Future in Space, (1994) commenting on a NASA photograph beamed back to earth from the spacecraft *Cassini* orbiting Saturn (3.7 billion miles) from Earth.

"Look again at that dot. That's here. That's home. That's us. On it everyone you love, everyone you know, everyone you ever heard of, every human being who ever was, lived out their lives. The aggregate of our joy and suffering, thousands of confident religions, ideologies, and economic doctrines, every hunter and forager, every hero and coward, every creator and destroyer of civilization, every king and peasant, every young couple in love, every mother and father, hopeful child, inventor and explorer, every teacher of morals, every corrupt politician, every 'superstar,' every 'supreme leader,' every saint and sinner in the history of our species lived there — on a mote of dust suspended in a sunbeam."

Epilogue

HUMANS ARE A curious lot. On the one hand we believe we have supernatural traits, but in reality, we are a natural product. It may not be obvious to all that our behavior is in some degree, maybe a great degree, dictated by the brain we inherited from earlier ancestors. That's not to say that we don't have a great capacity to learn and to make reasoned decisions. However, it is the brain that enabled *Homo sapiens* to be the last hominin standing.

It would be satisfying to present a master plan that would insure man's long term survival on Planet Earth. Obviously, this book was not intended as a 12 step improvement guide for humans. There are no easy solutions; they may be no practical solutions. Surprisingly, I am not a fatalist. I would call myself a realist. The future of mankind is unknowable, but there are indicators that we should pay attention. I don't have *thee* answer as to what life is. I'm still exploring; this book has been part of that exploration.

My aspiration for this book is to stimulate thought and discussion by highlighting our long history and selective human traits and behaviors. I challenged conservative values and from my liberal perspective have found them wanting, in terms of human survivability. Your perspective may differ. I am reasonably certain I will not have changed many behaviors or beliefs. Our political and religious views are deeply entrenched. Change is difficult.

However change is possible with education; a liberal education that encompasses the sciences and the humanities. We should know our history. We need to understand science and mathematics. We should all appreciate our cultural traditions of art, music and literature. We need to embrace, actively support, less costly higher education. Great expectations, yes; but if we are to become that *Nobel Species* we should become acutely aware of our place in the universe. I certainly can't predict what our future might be. However, we can strive to be respectful of all life and aspire to be more humane.

www.ingramcontent.com/pod-product-compliance
Lightning Source LLC
Chambersburg PA
CBHW060252050426
42448CB00009B/1622

9780615970097